The Book

That Takes You on a

FULFILLING

52-Week Getaway to Extraordinary Results

For Your Life!

INDELETHIO NEBEKER

Inspiring Indy

ISBN 978-1-0980-3133-6 (paperback)
ISBN 978-1-0980-3134-3 (digital)

Christian Faith Publishing, Inc.
832 Park Avenue
Meadville, PA 16335
www.christianfaithpublishing.com

Scripture quotations are from The Holy Bible www.Biblehub.com NIV Version (2019).

Printed in the United States of America

CONTENTS

Read This First

You hold in your hands **52 fantastically thought-provoking, achievement-generating exercises** for you to GET OUT OF YOUR HEAD AND INTO YOUR LIFE.

The directions are simple.

Read one exercise each week and follow the directions (for those of you who need to skip around, well then skip around; for those who like order, do them in order).

Please do not be afraid to write in the book!

You get to decide if and how to use the exercise in your life.

Do not over think the exercise.

Use the exercise for a positive result in your life.

Be open to exploration and new possibilities in your life.

Be positive about your expectations.

If you are so bold, invite someone to join you in working together through the exercises.

Have fun.

This is a culmination of over forty-four years of experience—trials, errors, success, failure, ups, downs, re-dos, winning, losing, laughing, crying, empowering, helping, dreaming, hoping.

Wherever this finds you in life, my wish is that it propels you to the next best chapter of your life!

WEEK 1

The Greatest Coaching Exercise You Will Ever Use

It is called the YES/NO Exercise.

I believe it is the ultimate "Get out of your head and into your life" application. Simply put, if you say YES to something in your schedule or your actions or decisions, you automatically are saying NO to something in return (and vise-versa). In your work life, if you say YES to that meeting or that project or that committee, what are you saying NO to? In your personal life, if you say YES to that relationship or eating decision or money spending action, what are you saying NO to? You do this a hundred, if not a thousand, times a day, but ARE YOU CONSCIOUSLY AWARE OF IT? Start today and become consciously aware of your decisions—in doing so, your choices and actions will become increasingly more impactful!

This week I will say YES to...
and therefore,
I will say NO to...

This week I will say NO to...
and therefore,
I will say YES to...

OR you can make yes/no affirmation statements for your week:
This week I say YES **to...**
This week I say NO **to...**

> **Remember**
> **Life is all about what**
> **choices we make...**
>
> **And it usually comes**
> **down to what we say**
> **YES or NO**
> **to.**
>
> #INSPIRINGINDY

WEEK 2

The Week of Mind-Dumping for Your Sanity

**Or what I like to call the Three
Columns to Success Exercise.**

The never-ending to-do list is swirling in your mind like a tornado.
You have projects, you have meetings, and you have individuals all
needing/wanting your time and you feel like you are drowning…

NOW IS THE TIME TO TAKE CONTROL!

This simple tool will get you started instantly and it only takes ten to fifteen minutes.

One rule: NO JUDGING. THE LIST DOES NOT NEED TO BE PERFECT (just start writing)!

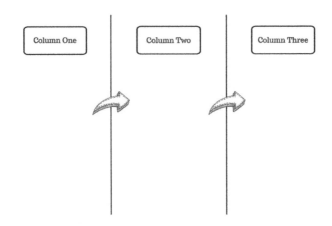

Step 1: Column 1 is the "MIND DUMP" Column. In bullet points, write down everything about your week that is swirling in your mind. Remember, *no judging*, just get it all written down in that first column. This step is crucial. Mind-dumping the items out of your head and onto the paper will help you start to reduce some of the anxiety you are feeling because you are no longer letting it swirl—YOU ARE TAKING CONTROL!

Step 2: Hopefully you have a list of at least seven to ten items. From the mind dump list, take the top five that seem to be screaming out at you AND WRITE THOSE TOP FIVE down in Column 2. I know, I know, *everything* on your mind dump list seems important to you; however, if *everything* on your list is important to you, then in reality, nothing is important to you. It is time to prioritize—you know which items are needing your attention. And don't worry, the items left in the mind dump list will be waiting for you.

Step 3: The Chosen. FROM COLUMN 2, CHOOSE THE TOP THREE that are *really screaming* out at you and WRITE THOSE THREE ITEMS down in Column 3. *This is your actual to-do-list.*

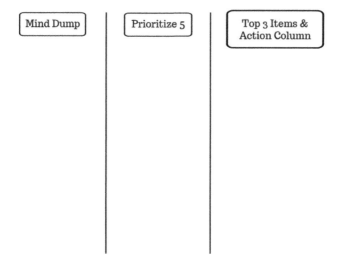

Step 4: Action time. Now that you have prioritized what needs your attention, it is time to TAKE ACTION. Write down one to three action bullet points under the priority item.

Column Three
Priority Item #1

- Action Step
- Action Step
- Action Step

Once you start knocking items off the list, re-organize the list and repeat the process. Also, you can use this tool with your team to have a highly-focused meeting and as a reference tool to keep everyone accountable.

Pro Tip: This is an excellent tool for teams or work groups to use in order to get everyone on the same page mentally. At the end of the planning session, everyone should have a dated copy to refer to, this will ensure accountability and point all team members in the same direction in terms of priority action items.

DO NOT OVER THINK THIS...START WRITING NOW.

Heads Up!
It Is Time to Exercise the Four
Features of Your Personality!

This week, we will start the four-week discovery into your inner personality. There are many personality-profile tools out there that you can use to uncover or discover your unique attributes, both positive and negative, that make up your personality. Ultimately, they usually melt down to four key types. And while it is easy to fall into the trap of saying, "I am who I am" and only focus on your strengths and natural tendencies, I remind my leadership clients that to truly be successful one needs to understand ALL of the four types in order to make THEIR LEADERSHIP LASTING AND IMPACTFUL.

This was brought to light in a coaching session I had with a hospital executive who was very detailed oriented, reserved, and did not always see the need for emotional connection. In giving presentations, this executive would often times find themselves walking away only partly satisfied and wondering why they struggled to get the response for their project they were seeking. I pointed out that they were leaving part of their power outside of the room because they were only presenting with their detail-oriented personality and that not only does everyone have four parts to their personality, but NOT EVERYONE is detail-oriented first like them. The "lightbulb" went off when my client realized they may be only connecting with one-fourth of their audience!

Those with
High Emotional Intelligence
understand not only their own personality traits, but also the personality traits of others.

¥INSPIRINGINDY

WEEK 3

Discover Your "Inner Lead Dog"

Sometimes there are opportunities to show that you are "going for victory" and still other opportunities that need YOU to stand up and say, "This is the way" when others are unwilling or scared to do so. By working on your "Inner Lead Dog," you will begin to build a strength from within yourself you didn't realize you had and quite possibly one that others have been waiting to show up.

IMPORTANT NOTE: IF YOU ALREADY FIND THESE TRAITS NATURAL TO YOU, PAY ATTENTION TO HOW YOU CAN STAY IN BALANCE WITH THEM AND NOT BE OVER-THE-TOP OR OVERBEARING WITH THEM.

This week focus on:

- Going for the WIN
- Taking control
- Being decisive
- Being brave
- Having self-assurance (not everyone has to agree with you all the time)
- Being direct (Let your yes be yes and your no be no)
- A willingness to lead not just follow
- Having laser focus and taking action
- Watch the movie *Money Ball* starring Brad Pitt or *The Blind Side* staring Sandra Bullock

I will find my "Inner Lead Dog" this week by...

WEEK 4

Discover Your "Inner Energizing Honey Bee"

Think about the honey bee for a quick second. Does it sit in the hive all day and wait around for life to happen? Absolutely NOT! IT GETS TO WORK. PART OF THAT WORK ENTAILS GOING OUT OF THE HIVE AND VISITING ALL KINDS OF PLANTS AND FLOWERS to gather nectar and pollen. Inevitably, those bees rub off excess pollen on the flowers they visit and in turn fertilize the flower which then becomes a fruit or vegetable in most cases. The world would be without a lot of wonderful fruits, vegetables, and flowers if the bee just stayed in the hive all day long.

Get the point?

The world needs you to get out there and start "rubbing elbows" as they say. **People need to experience you and you need to experience them.** Yes, sometimes people will drive you crazy. Full stop. They can be downright agonizing. If that happens, be like the bee AND MOVE ON TO THE NEXT ONE! A new, possibly life-changing experience is around the corner waiting for you.

> IMPORTANT NOTE: IF YOU ALREADY FIND THESE TRAITS NATURAL TO YOU, PAY ATTENTION TO HOW YOU CAN STAY IN BALANCE WITH THEM AND NOT BE OVER-THE-TOP OR OVERBEARING WITH THEM.

This week focus on:

- Being curious rather than critical; curiosity is the driver of innovation
- Trying something new with an open mind, as I heard an Irish woman in New York City once say, **"Push the boat out honey!"**
- Fun!
- Saying "Hi" to people. If this is too big a step, then may I suggest offering a simple smile.
- Adjusting. Structure is fantastic, but be willing to deviate from your routine response or schedule this week
- Getting out of "the hive" whatever that means to you
- Watch the movie *Stranger Than Fiction* starring Will Ferrell

I will find my "Inner Energizing Honey Bee" this week by…

WEEK 5

Discover Your "Inner Oasis Superpowers"

What do you think of when you hear or say the word *oasis*? I envision
being completely parched, exhausted, and without hope, but then a

glimmer of optimism appears on the horizon to quench my draught. I visualize a healing lifeline picking me up after physical and mental struggles have taken their toll. I imagine a shadowy abyss full of loneliness only to be offered a hand that says, "How can I help you get back on your journey?"

Offered hands, lifelines, glimmers of optimism, helping without boasting, rejuvenation not transactions, possibility rather than criticizing—each offer the currency they both crave and operate from in the form of stability, cooperation, and, kindness. The magic of the "Oasis Superpower"? It receives its wealth as it gives from its depth.

IMPORTANT NOTE: IF YOU ALREADY FIND THESE TRAITS NATURAL TO YOU, PAY ATTENTION TO HOW YOU CAN STAY IN BALANCE WITH THEM AND NOT BE OVER-THE-TOP OR OVERBEARING WITH THEM.

This week focus on:

- Stopping to listen
- Offering a hand of help
- Connecting not just transacting
- Seek opportunities to offer acts of kindness
- Peacemaking
- Letting someone else go first
- Forgiving rather than being critical
- Stopping to listen, yes, again
- Watch the movie *Gandhi*

I will find my "Inner Oasis Superpower" this week by...

WEEK 6

Discover Your "Inner Quality Control"

This week is about precision and taking note of QUALITY not quantity. If you chose one or two things to focus on and do very well, what would those be? If you allowed yourself to notice details and not run them over, what would be the change to your daily experience?

And if you put value on your decision making, how would that be expressed in your life?

When you use your "Inner Quality Control," you will notice that opportunities for boundaries will appear. Is there anywhere you could use positive boundaries that would keep you on the path to success? What do those boundaries look like? And remember, with any respectful "Quality Control" precision is key and doing the job *well* is mandatory.

> **IMPORTANT NOTE:** IF YOU ALREADY FIND THESE TRAITS NATURAL TO YOU, PAY ATTENTION TO HOW YOU CAN STAY IN BALANCE WITH THEM AND NOT BE OVER-THE-TOP OR OVERBEARING WITH THEM.

This week focus on:

- The details
- Being composed vs. reactionary
- Analyzing before committing
- Being logical vs. emotional
- Collecting more data before making the decision
- Developing a deeper competency in an area of interest
- Quality, not quantity
- The male and female characters in the James Bond movie *Casino Royal* come to mind, as well as Ben Affleck's character in *The Accountant*

I will find my "Inner Quality Control" this week by...

WEEK 7

This Week Is "Set Up Your Sanctuary" Week

Do you have a space that is dedicated all to you?

I am talking about a space that is clutter-free, inviting, and yours. Yours to be free in. Yours to think in. Yours to create in. Yours to be **A SANCTUARY SPACE**.

My space is my bedroom. And I love it.

My wife and I have made our bedroom a special place. We repainted the walls a light and airy bluish-grey. We bought a new bed with a very inviting headboard. My wife found two lampstand drawers and had them painted a simple yet elegant white. I found lamps with sophisticated, easy pull-down strings to adorn each drawer. The windows are draped in cloth drapes and roman shades. Our bed is covered and routinely made with a majestic comforter and pillows.

Beside the bed is a "reading chair" next to the alluring light from the lamp on my side of the bed. We also have enough room for a cherished book shelf for my "important books" and a desk for our computer where we create—I write and my wife with her photography.

Adding to the senses, we seek out various scents to fill our room. Past favorites include Midsummer's Night Yankee Candles, Sleep Pillow Mist of Lavender and Chamomile and Blue Ocean Wave sprays from Bath & Body Works.

Not to be outdone, we seek out various soothing sounds to accompany our creative journeys; lately it is any variation of Bach—Cello Suite No. 1 in G Major.

It is our sanctuary.

Yes, enemies lurk to invade the space—clothes, kids bringing in toys, dust, daily messed up bed covers—however, this is a SANCTUARY. Any clutter is not allowed in the room to stay and therefore, the room is protected. I actively make sure this room is clean, clutter-free, safe, and soothing. Not surprisingly, our kids absolutely LOVE coming in to lay on our bed just to hang out—it is an inviting space.

Do you see the elements at work here?

A space, whatever the size.

Furniture or pieces that inspire your creativity.

Stirring your senses—touch, smell, and sound.

Simple and clutter free. Protected. Yours.

Hear now from Anya Nebeker, Baby Whisperer of Geaux Smile Photography:

> You go about your day around the house like your normal self...but then something transforms. You go through the door of your "sanctuary" like there is a magical curtain that transforms you from the usual you to an ARTIST/CREATOR/ PAINTER/SCIENTIST or whoever you want to be— it is a different dimension of your usual self that you don't always present, but it is something unique that you have to offer the world.

This week I will start to create a "Sanctuary Space" by:

Create
Your
Sanctuary
Place

WEEK 8

Your "Kick-Starter for Life" Roadmap!

Have you ever had feelings like you needed a "do-over?" Or maybe you have feelings like you are lost at sea with ideas but are overwhelmed with where or how to start? This week is simplified down to one question: ***What would it look like if you "reinvented" yourself?***

I have had to "reinvent" myself several times over the years. Whether it was in my twenties figuring out a direction to start my life's journey and career by moving to New York City or in my thirties going through cancer and then a divorce or even now, in my mid-forties settling in on my experience and transferring my consulting and leadership—I am a "reinventor" of myself. One of my top ways of getting this process started is by brainstorming or writing out my "Kickstarter" Roadmap. It is very similar to the "Three Columns to Success" exercise a couple of weeks back, however, this week we are only focused on writing out the first column, which I call the "Dream Column." Do yourself and others around you a favor and stop the madness of your ideas swirling in your head AND WRITE THEM DOWN in a bullet point format. And as a reminder, one rule—DO NOT JUDGE THE ROADMAP!

The roadmap does not need to be "perfect" or "right" or even possible right now. If this week's exercise resonates with you, it is probably because your world might be a little upside-down, not exactly where you envisioned and needing a boost, am I right? So if this is true, how could your map be even close to being the "right map" right now?

And it does not need to be.

Just get the map started; it's a starting point and definitely not an ending point. To push this idea further, I am reminded of a hilarious saying I heard during a night out on the town with my much older workmates from one of my first jobs when drinking and navigating through crowds of people: "Indy, just like in life, **it's forward, never straight. Now onward!**"

REMINDER:

Your "Road Map" does not need to be perfect...just get started!

This is what my roadmap looked like at age thirty-seven when I was alone (I was going through a divorce) and had serious financial difficulties (I just got finished going through a battle with cancer and had not worked fully for close to two years).

- *Buy new clothes*
    I ended up buying two pairs of new pants, five new shirts, and one pair of new shoes
- *Learn to dance Salsa*
    this ended up turning into Argentine tango dancing instead, and I became obsessed for about three years
- *Lose twenty pounds*
    This turned into losing more like sixty pounds. I went from 236lbs to 175lbs.
- *Start cooking Thai food*
    I never did this one. I ate at Thai restaurants from time to time.
- *Buy my own house*
    This was a joke in my mind when I wrote it, but four years later I purchased my FIRST HOUSE!
- *Buy a boat*
    Again, this was a joke in my mind when I wrote it down, but four years later I purchased my FIRST BOAT!
- *Read the Bible more*
    THIS! Actually, this whole time in my life was what I believe to be GOD melting me down in order to build me back up. HE was calling me, and I finally realized I needed to invite HIM into my pain, sadness, and loneliness. The way that looked in my life was by reading the Bible, praying and crying out to God daily, and going to church on a more consistent basis. I will never forget the day I prayed that GOD would make everything I had in my life new and then threw my old wedding band out of my truck window over the Causeway Bridge into Lake Pontchartrian. Since that day, over ten years ago, literally EVERYTHING in my life is new.

28

- *Start writing*

  I ended up self-publishing a book called Toxic Ingredients: The Top 10 Factors That Get Your Kid in Trouble. *Look it up on Amazon.*
- *Go on a trip by myself*

  This turned into an unimaginable trip to the Philippines where I met my NEW WIFE!

One More Time:

Your "Road Map" does not need to be perfect...

Just get started!

Write your roadmap!

My Kick-Starter for Life Roadmap   Date:
(START WRITING NOW! DO NOT OVER-THINK THIS!)

WEEK 9

30-Minutes of Self Care

Fifteen years of coaching individuals, and this is **one of the BIGGEST challenges** I have listened to from people on all levels—**taking time to take care of ourselves.** There are some personalities out in the world that are highly driven and seemingly successful in financial terms but almost bankrupt mentally and emotionally. The pitfall for these types is to be constantly "doing" with the perception being if I am actively working, I am therefore winning. Still there are other personality types that are very giving of themselves and their time to others. They are seemingly successful with the number of friends and fun they have, but again they are emotionally and mentally bankrupt. These constant "doings" finally pay a toll on both of these personalities if they do not take time to stop and recharge.

Have you noticed you have a shorter "fuse" or temper with people?

You need 30 minutes of self-care!

Trouble coping with stressful situations?

You need 30 minutes of self-care!

Feeling "burnt out" because you feel all you do is give but not receive?

You need 30 minutes of self-care!

Here is a point most individuals do not think of because they are "too busy" to take time: by actually doing your 30 minutes of self-care, you will be BETTER when you re-engage in your normal routines and responsibilities. You will have new energy and stamina because you have rested those "emotional muscles" that have been constantly flexed and used.

Your 30 minutes of self-care does not need to be earth shattering. It does not need to be an over-the-top experience.

Keep it simple.

It does, however, need to be an activity removed from your everyday routine and responsibilities. This is the only rule for your 30 minutes of self-care. Re-read it and stick to it. So yes, that means if your everyday routine consists of doing things with your family or for your children, THAT DOES NOT COUNT FOR YOUR 30 MINUTES OF SELF-CARE!

Remember, by actually sticking to your 30 minutes of self-care, you will actually be BETTER for your family, your spouse, your coworkers, your clients, etc. when you re-engage. These people are important to you, right? Then take care of yourself!

This week for my "30 Minutes of Self-Care," I will do:

If you cannot take
30 Minutes for
yourself...
It is a sign that you are
probably not being
efficient in other places
of your life.

 #INSPIRINGINDY

WEEK 10

How is it showing up in your daily routine?

Use YES/NO as a filter in order to make your decisions that much more impactful!

This week I will say YES to...
and therefore, I will say NO to...

This week I will say NO to…
And therefore, I will say YES to…

Or you can make YES/NO affirmation statements for your week:
This week I say YES to…
This week I say NO to…

> **Remember**
> **Life is all about what**
> **choices we make…**
>
> **And it usually comes**
> **down to what we say**
> **YES or NO**
> **to.**
>
> #INSPIRINGINDY

WEEK 11

The Shut Up And Listen Week

This is called turning off your "first-person voice."

What is your "first-person voice"?
It is the voice filled with "I" and "me"

35

I feel...
I like...
I want...
I do not like...
I need...
That doesn't work for me...
My idea is...
What I think is...

Do you get the point? It is your self-centered voice. It is your narcissistic voice. It is your narrow-view voice. It is your waiting to talk, not really listening voice. And it is missing possibilities for success because its volume is turned up *too high*.

Here is a simple example I give in presentations to demonstrate:

Me: What is your favorite food?

Participant: Um, I guess if I had to choose it would be chocolate ice cream.

Me: (almost interrupting) Really? Wow, I really don't like chocolate ice cream because there was this one time when...

Do you see what happened? Do you see how my "first-person voice" took over the *other person's* experience? Do you think they felt heard or listened to? Do you think there was much connection happening? This happens all of the time in our interactions. We (or others who we are interacting with) immediately put OUR OWN "FIRST PERSON" experience over the other person's experience, and this totally shuts the connecting process down. The result? We miss opportunities.

Does this mean you cannot have an opinion? No. Does it mean that you have to agree with what the other person is saying or feeling? Of course not. However, the point is to not let this be your go-to mechanism for interaction if you want to connect on a higher level. (You will probably start to hate me now because you will notice how many people are stuck in "FIRST PERSON LISTENING" ALL OF THE TIME!)

We all walk around in our "first-person voice," it is only natural. However, to be a LEADER, to be more powerful with our communication, to truly connect, we need to turn down the volume of our

"FIRST PERSON voice" and GET CURIOUS about our surroundings, the other person in front of us, and the moment at hand. By doing so, *you will allow for more information to flow to you which can ultimately give you more power in your decisions and actions.*

To drive this point even further, I want to circle back to the ice cream question. I could hate ice cream. I could be allergic to ice cream. I could have had a terrible experience with ice cream growing up as a kid. All that being said, I can still connect with the other person by get curious about THEIR EXPERIENCE with the ice cream by turning down my "FIRST PERSON VOICE" and seeking to understand them.

This week, I will turn my "FIRST PERSON" voice down by:

WEEK 12

This Is the Week of Using Your Hands to Create and Touch Lives

I make biscuits.

There is a certain distinct pleasure in mixing ingredients to make a dough which then translates into something I can contribute and/or nourish my body.

Do you see the elements at play here?

Mixing. Creating. Sharing. Eating.

It is a rich environment, both complex in subtleties and simple in delivery.

The process of crafting something and seeing it come to fruition is so satisfying. Sadly, I believe it is deeply craved and yet lost in today's technological abyss. The dough forming through your fingers and then pressed into shape. Heat solidifying the shape into a flavor that can be met with so many possible outcomes.

Thick, fluffy mountains sliced in half with melted butter slathered on each inner side. Add a sweetness if you prefer of honey or the fruit preserves of your choice (I love blackberry). How about these savory morsels topped with a gravy just infused with the latest drippings of roasted pork, chicken, or that bacon that you just fried up? Do you like fruit? Mix frozen blueberries in your dough and finish off with a lemon glaze immediately after removing from the oven. And move over fast food restaurants. They will have *nothing* on your homemade ham, cheese, and egg biscuit sensation.

And if you are doing this all alone, you are doing it wrong. I leave just enough dough for my three-year-old daughter to roll out and shape into her own "fish bickets," as she calls them. These tiny delights get baked in the remaining heat after the first batch of biscuits are completed. I have also taught my three older sons from start to finish the required ingredients and steps so that "they can always know how to bake something from scratch for themselves." I am proud to say that my eldest has already embarked on the tradition himself and texts me pictures of his final trophies. Do yourself a favor, involve others in your process.

And the pièce de résistance—the taste! What is better than sitting down and sharing in the eating of your own handiwork with others? Delightful. Rewarding. Satisfying. And yes, filling. You certainly do not achieve these lasting impressions from the already processed can or fast food lane. And thank goodness there is no one-button computer app to attempt to steal the moment of satisfaction. Nope, with biscuits, one must go through each simple step in order to achieve greatness.

One more thing. Do not forget the lagniappe element that underlines the whole process—time. Time well spent, if you allow it. You will have to see for yourself.

This week I will use my hands to create and share by:

And if you think of it, I would love to see a picture of your "biscuits" so post some and tag me **#inspiringindythelightbulbcoach** so we can see it!

REMINDER:

**Do not let
Convenience steal
from your
Experience &
Memories!**

#INSPIRINGINDY

WEEK 13

Your Positive Action Plan Accelerator Week

By now, you have written out a couple of action items lists for a possible positive future. Maybe you have started to move forward on them, maybe you haven't. This week I am reminding you about those points of possibility and will empower you to engage if you haven't already.

Step 1

Fill in the goal wheel with **four goals or areas of your life** you want to focus on.

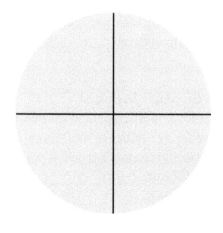

Step 2

Plug in one of those goals or areas that you want to focus on in the Action Plan Accelerator Tool:

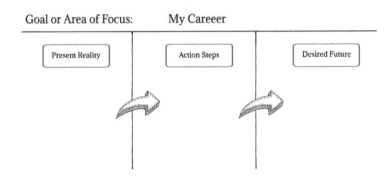

Goal or Area of Focus: My Careeer

| Present Reality | Action Steps | Desired Future |

Step 3

Pick an entry point. You can either start with the "present reality" or "desired future," you get to decide.

For example, if I chose "present reality" first, I would start to bullet point the present reality of my current career position—my likes, dislikes, feelings, etc. Any and all pertinent information regarding the "present reality" would go in that column.

Next, I would then proceed to the "desired future" column and bullet-point all of the ideas and thoughts I wanted from the "goal or action area" I was focusing on. In this case, I would write out my "desired future" regarding my career.

Step 4

This is where the magic happens!

By looking at the gap or discrepancy between your "present reality" and your "desire future" bullet points, you will almost instantly see what possible ACTION STEPS you need to take in order to get from your "present" to your "future"!

You know who you are.

Deep down, you know exactly what steps you need to start doing. Write those down in the "ACTION STEPS" column. If by chance you struggle with this, ask yourself:

What am I willing to do to get from my "present reality" to my "desired future"?

Write it down!

You now are equipped with a unique action plan tailored specifically to your goal or action area of your life.

And remember, the more detail or specific the action item, the more likely it is you will achieve success in the "action area." Ideally, you will have three to five action steps written out.

Pro Tip: Get a partner and take turns talking out each step with one another until each of you has at least one Action Plan Accelerator completely filled out.

> **This is only a piece of paper. NONE of your success will happen if all you do is let the paper sit...**
> **Get into Action Now!**
>
> #INSPIRINGINDY

Scoreboard

This is your 1st Quarter Check-up. How are you doing so far with each exercise?

- ☐ Week 1: The Greatest Coaching Exercise You Will Ever Use
- ☐ Week 2: Mind Dumping for Your Sanity
- ☐ Week 3: Find Your Inner Lead Dog
- ☐ Week 4: Find Your Inner Honey Bee
- ☐ Week 5: Find Your Inner Oasis Super Powers
- ☐ Week 6: Find You Inner Quality Control
- ☐ Week 7: Set Up Your Sanctuary
- ☐ Week 8: Kickstarter for Life Roadmap
- ☐ Week 9: 30 Minutes of Self-Care
- ☐ Week 10: Yes/No Exercise
- ☐ Week 11: Shut Up and Listen
- ☐ Week 12: Use Your Hands to Create and Touch Lives
- ☐ Week 13: The Action Plan Accelerator

WEEK 14

Smell the Flowers & Blow Out the Candles

When I was in New York City embarking on my acting phase, I took a lot of different acting classes. Of those acting classes a couple were voice classes. In one such class, we would take about twenty minutes to warm up and "get grounded" in order to be ready to fully use our voices to their potential. I will never forget lying on the floor with my eyes closed and being told to have my "mind's eye" send my legs like roots to the center of the earth and my neck and spine to reach up into the middle of the universe. Take a guess what the mechanism was to reach such depths and heights for our visionary journey. Yep, you guessed it—our breath. We were instructed to breathe as deeply as we could and with each exhale we would stretch that much further to our enchanted goal.

It was intoxicating.

Deep, meaningful breathing.

And to my surprise, it was both relaxing AND energizing.

At that time, in my twenties, focusing on my breath wasn't something I did on a conscious, deliberate level. But of course, it makes sense. Delivering that much oxygen to your muscles and organs certainly won't make you lethargic. The whole idea of the warm up was to get us ready to perform, not put us to sleep. The deep breathing opened us up internally so that we could use our bodies and voices freely without hindrance and at the same time ground our minds so that we could be keenly focused and tuned in to our performance.

Think of these words and breathe deeply as you read each one. Take a few moments for each word:

Relaxed... In control... Free...Energized... Grounded... Focused... My Performance...

Over the years I have had many people ask me for help when it comes to public speaking. One of the first items I will start to talk to them about is their breathing. Not only will deep breathing help calm you down when your nerves start to kick in, it will also energize your voice when you take the stage. Do you want your first sentence to come out strong? Take a breath deep into your stomach, not your chest, and your delivery will come out solid.

Have you ever noticed the "nervous twitchier"? That person who cannot stop fidgeting with their pen or can't stop shaking their leg at the table in the meeting? Or have you noticed even yourself in stressful situations feeling like your muscles are tensing up? Personally, my tense spot is in my legs. I have noticed over the years that when I am in a stressful moment my thighs tend to tighten up. However, because of my breathing awareness, I am able to remind myself to relax my legs and "breathe into my legs" to release the tension. It works every single time.

This week engage in deep, meaningful breathing.

Use your breath to calm yourself down before you fall asleep. Use your breath to center you in the moment. Use your breath to inhale positive ideas and emotions. Use your breath to exhale negative thoughts away from your mind and body. Use your breath to engage in listening—listening to others, your surroundings, and yourself.

Use your breath to energize your mind and your body.

Hear from Nicole Azzi, Co-owner of Bayou Yoga and Expert Yoga instructor:

> Strengthening the use of your breath, training the logical mind (the brain) to stay tuned into breath can help keep you "out of your head." With the sensations of the body at the forefront of our thoughts and reactions, we can control the direction our thoughts go into simply by learning to recognize the patterns we fall in to when faced with people and events that serve as our triggers. Once you learn your patterns, you can use the power and the awareness of your breath to re-imprint and re-direct your thoughts and behaviors.

PRO TIP: Help children "smell the flowers and blow out the candles" when they are upset by physically inhaling and exhaling with them while saying the words, "Smell the flowers (inhale)…blow out the candles (exhale)." Repeat in a soothing manner until they calm down.

This week I will use deep, meaningful breathing to:

Take a
Deep Cleansing
Breath Now...

#INSPIRINGINDY

WEEK 15

This Week Fill in Someone Else's "Emotional Piggy Bank"

A common theme that comes up with my coaching clients is motivating direct reports. I am often asked about ideas and best practices when it comes to motivating employees. There are many resources out there to give you all kinds of ideas, but I caution my clients that there isn't a magic pill out there that fits all situations.

People Don't Care What You Know Until They Know You Care

You've heard that one before, and it's true, especially when it comes to motivating people. If you open up page 36 of some random leadership book and say, "Hey, I think I'll try this one," your people will see right through it unless, of course, it genuinely connects to your audience.

I'm reminded of a story about an NFL football team. I believe it was the New York Giants, and how the defensive lineman coach motivated his group of players for practice. His big question was, "How does one motivate a bunch of millionaires?" Turns out the answer was through Twinkies. Whoever won the drill of the day was that day's "King of the Twinkie"! The players loved it. They ate it up—literally and figuratively. That coach knew his audience well.

Walking Emotional Piggy Banks

In most cases, workplace leaders do not have a practice field where all of their "players" get to perform in front of them. In fact, because of technology, direct reports may be in other buildings, cities, or even countries working remotely. This makes the leader's job even more challenging in terms of motivating. Ironically, it takes self-motivation on the leader's part to stay on top of the concept I like to call "filling up the emotional piggy bank" of others.

As leaders, we all need to call upon people at one point or another to dig in, put forth extra effort, strive for that goal. Sometimes morale is low because of overburdened employees, being over budget, or turnover is high within a department. Or it may just come down to one day you, as a leader, may need a favor from someone because you are stretched too thin. Whatever the case, the concept of "fill emotional piggy banks" of those around you is the place to start in terms of motivating people.

1. **Become aware of opportunity.**
   Look at the people around you. There are people who (a) you report to (b) they report to you or (c) you may need something from them in the future. Whatever the scenario may be, THEY ALL HAVE AN EMOTIONAL PIGGY BANKS INSIDE OF THEM.

2. **Deposits or withdrawals?**
   What we are really talking about is influence. Is your influence of people attracting or detracting? Again, look at the people around you. Are you asking from these people or are you investing in these people? Asking = withdrawal, investing = deposit. IF THE EMOTIONAL PIGGY BANK IS NOT FULL OF DEPOSITS, MAKING WITHDRAWALS IS VERY DIFFI-CULT! In the end, it is all about how we are or are not influencing people. If we want to lead with transformation, that is, leadership that leaves a lasting impact, we must have emotion deposits built up within those we want to influence the most.

3. **Investing?**
   When it comes to investing in people, money goes a certain distance, but time is what really counts. I remind my clients that the more personal the deposits are, the bigger the return will be. Sometimes all it takes is a quick text or email, however these are small deposits. A next level deposit is a phone call. And the biggest deposit of all is? You guessed it! FACE-TO-FACE!

4. **But how?**
   One day you will need to make a withdrawal from someone's "emotional piggy bank," so it better be filled in order for your success rate to be high. But how do we make

deposits? I've always liked the phrase "Come from contribution." Genuinely get interested in your audience and your action will be appropriate. Get curious about them. Say "Hi" to them without that reason being because something is wrong in the department. "Catch" them doing something well and point it out. And when in doubt, use this opening line: *"I was thinking about you and/so..."* It is genuine, and it works every single time.

Of course, this is not regulated to just work-related people. Everyone—and I mean everyone—you have in your life, whether it is a close friend, family member, forgotten friend, or someone you just bumped into, they all have an "emotional piggy bank" inside of them. The question is, will you be withdrawing from it or depositing from it? If you bring your awareness here, you will become very powerful in your relationships and influence.

Pro Tip: The side benefit of "filling an emotional piggy bank" is you will probably feel great inside too!

THIS WEEK'S CHALLENGE:
THIS WEEK, PICK OUT 3 PEOPLE AND FILL THEIR EMOTIONAL PIGGY BANK.

WEEK 16

30 Minutes of Self-Care This Week

Again, as a reminder, fifteen years of coaching individuals and this is one of the BIGGEST challenges I have listened to from people on all levels—taking time to take care of ourselves.

This week I am going to encourage you to do a simple task in order to take care of yourself:

DRINK WATER.

Your body does not need coffee. It does, however, NEED WATER.

Your body does not need diet soft drinks. It does, however, NEED WATER.

Your body does not need wine or beer. It does, however, NEED WATER.

Do you see what is going on here?

How many times have you tricked yourself into thinking you "needed" something and therefore made it into a habit?

"I need a cup of coffee in the morning otherwise I can't function."

"I have to have my diet (fill in your favorite) before I can even think about starting…"

"I usually need a few drinks in me in order to get up the courage to…"

LIES.

ALL LIES.

Language can be a powerful trap that ensnares us to certain behaviors, so I want you to start bringing your awareness to your daily language and take control of your choices.

Personally, I love coffee. Are you kidding me? New Orleans style coffee with the chicory and warm milk? Yes please! However, I am not ruled by it. I also control what I put into it. Years ago, I stopped adding sugar. I still love it without the added calories and on my own terms.

Beer? Hello! With the rise of the many local brews almost everywhere you travel, it's a fun way to taste your way through a trip. The same is true with wine. What a celebration in a glass! And that is exactly what it is, isn't it? A celebration with friends, with family, and if I am drunk all of the time, I am missing the experience and missing the point. I truly do not want to make the things I celebrate with to become my master—which brings me back to water.

Water is nourishing and cleansing—drink a glass or two to detox your system.

It can be used as a buffer in place of added extra calories. Instead of taking the larger portion of food or extra helping of food, drink a glass of water as an actual part of the meal.

And who doesn't want to take care of their skin better? Drinking water is one of the best ways to keep your skin looking fresh and young.

Need some flavor?

Guide your body to enjoy tea (just don't add sugar). There is just something about a hot cup of peppermint tea that has a soothing quality about it. Or a lemon/berry tea iced down in the middle of a hot day is just so refreshing.

Water is a natural way of telling your body I LOVE YOU. So grab a glass and relish the moment of taking care of yourself. There are so many positive benefits to enjoy. And when you do, if you think of me, take a picture and send it to my Inspiring Indy Facebook page or tag us with **#inspiringindy**.

Let's enjoy this together!

This week, for my "30 minutes of self-care," I will:

WEEK 17

This Week Become a Creative Master Through the Chaos

Or as I like to call it, the Chef Massimo Bottura exercise, "Oops I dropped the lemon tart!"

From one Netflix episode of *Chef's Table*, I became an instant fan of Massimo Bottura. You may too.

The night was almost over. Two last guests in the restaurant ordered the last two remaining lemon tarts, a pleasant end to a busy evening of dining. And then catastrophe—one of the tarts being plated by the sous chef inexplicably fell off the plate and was splattered all over the kitchen counter (I have worked in restaurants before—sheer panic takes over the surrounding area for sure)! However, on this night, the magic, leadership, and inspiration that is Chef Massimo Bottura took over. Instead of blowing the proverbial gasket and humiliating his staff, Chef Massimo saw opportunity and seized the moment.

Take the Present Ingredients and See Something New

"Freeze! Let's capture that!" His idea was simple and genius all in one. Chef Massimo instructed his staff to "capture the moment" as if they were taking a snapshot of it and then recreating the "catastrophe" on a plate. In essence, they deconstructed the lemon tart by splashing the individual ingredients on a plate with the result being "Oops, I dropped the lemon tart!" It is now one of the restaurant's signature dishes.

Deconstructing the "Ingredients" for New Solutions

Often in my coaching calls, I find myself helping my clients brainstorm through various challenges and problems. It is a process of going from mental block to possibility. From the example of the lemon tart, we can glean some approaches that can be used to do just that.

1. **It's called reframing.** Sometimes all that is needed is a new perspective to see the challenge at hand in a new light. Reframing is not intuitive for most and requires in some cases new training of the mind to allow oneself to step out of their chaos/stress moment.

2. **How?** Take the present elements of the situation and seek to view them from a different vantage point. Consider:
   - **Our view vs. the client's view**
   - **The everyday user vs. the new user**
   - **Traditional vs. nontraditional**

   In the story, the chef made a decision of going with a nontraditional presentation of a classic dessert to come up with a new solution.

3. **Start to ask new questions of those elements by coming from a place of curiosity:**
   - Why do we do it that way?
   - What if we changed (add to or eliminate) this element of the process?
   - Where have we become complacent?
   - Who are new players we can involve?
   - Has the landscape changed?

   By deconstructing the lemon tart, Chef Massimo Bottura highlighted and accented each ingredient which brought a greater sensual arousal and culinary experience for his guests.

Perspective—it's all in how you are looking at it.

How often in our lives don't we find ourselves trying to figure out some sort of solution to a problem? With our clients, it may be looking at their bottom lines, with our staff or coworkers some version of a conflict resolution or even with our spouse or children there always seems to be a riddle of sort to figure out. From observation and my own experience, I find that the solutions we gravitate toward do not go much further than that of our own sphere of influence, that is to say, our perspective from which we look at life. In short, we get lazy or just stuck in our ways and then find ourselves stuck at a dead end of no solutions at all.

A couple of years ago when my eldest son was a bit younger, he wanted me to play Legos with him. His main goal in playing with the Legos that day was to build a bridge for his train and he enlisted me to help. As we were playing and putting the pieces together, it became very apparent rather quickly (to me) that we were not going to have enough Legos to finish the job. I pointed this out to my son with the resignation that we were going to have to stop because "it wasn't going to work."

Without flinching or pausing, my son started introducing new materials to our bridge—a shoe, a cereal box, a track from another toy set, I think even one of his younger brother's diapers were used. "See, Daddy, we still can make our bridge…" Yep, I had us stuck at the dead end of solutions because of my perspective. My perspective put rules around the making of our bridge and therefore stopped its production. My son on the other hand finished the job because he did not hinder his creativity when seeking the solution. Sometimes the solutions to our chaos are just outside of our usual choices. Let this be a reminder: maybe it's time to look a litter further and check your perspective!

From time to time, we find not only ourselves but those we lead, falling into mental ruts and the mundane day-to-day process of the work grind. Consider asking yourself, "Is there another perspective to try here?" or use the "Oops, I dropped the lemon tart" experience in both your work and personal life, as it may pave the way for some new, exciting opportunities to operate out of in your life and out of the chaos.

Pro Tip: Search out Chef Massimo Bottura on the Web or Netflix. He is truly an inspiration.

This week, I will use the "Oops, I dropped the lemon tart" experience by:

Perspectives are like glasses...

Be willing to try a few on before making your final decision.

 #INSPIRINGINDY

WEEK 18

This Week I Want You to Write a Letter to Yourself

Then I want you to read the letter in a year. This will be an incredible gift to yourself. Trust me.

Writing a letter to yourself is like writing out the ultimate "goal list" only in story form. That future date when you re-read it will be a reminder from the heart—your heart. That day will be a victory dance to celebrate the distance you covered in determination. Or it may very well be a mirror reflecting back to you the steps needed or once desired to get you back on track. Do not wait for the "perfect" time to write out the letter—you need to establish some sort of base line, otherwise you will not see any growth once you re-read your letter.

Take the time to write this gift out now.

This is what my gift looked like:

Dec 2014
Nice work, WARRIOR!

- **You married the dream girl :)**
- **You didn't let $ money sabotage you :)**
- **Guess what? You actually made the $150K that we put on the plan for 2014!**
- **Remember I told you someone was going to present you with an opportunity to truly use your leadership skills and get paid. Remember? Well, that happened too :)**

I love you,
Your Warrior,
Indelethio

Ps. It was worth it, wasn't it? :)

That was a short bullet-point letter to myself (apparently l enjoy bullet points).

May I also suggest as an idea to get you started for a maximized experience using this simple format:

1. Paragraph one talk about the PAST.
2. Paragraph two talk about the PRESENT.
3. Paragraph three talk about the FUTURE.

4.	Don't forget to say good bye and sign the letter.
5.	And don't forget to date the letter.

When you are finished, seal the letter up and put it somewhere for safe keeping. Read in one year.

Pro Tip: Put the letter in a self-addressed stamped envelope and have someone else send it to you in a year.

Write your letter (Don't overthink this).

WEEK 19

The Week of Stealthy Ninja Communication

This week I want you to communicate on a whole other level. And when I say, "whole other level," what I really mean to say is **I want you to WIN in your conversations.**

I want you to win with a stealth that conquers the other side without them noticing while simultaneously allowing you to collect what it is you need from the situation.

I want your communication style to be so engaging that it is both directive and nonconfrontational all at once. I want you to engage others to do the "work" in the conversation so that you can be the conductor actively directing the path of the discussion. I want you to gain full access to a flow of information in such a manner that the other person shows you their "bull's-eye" in any dialogue.

I want you to be a ninja in your communicating.

In his highly recommended book, *Never Split the Difference*, author Chris Voss refers to this type of communicating as "tactile empathy."

The bottom-line result? You will gain influence with whomever you are engaging in order to put YOU IN THE DRIVER'S SEAT OF THE CONVERSATION.

How?

With one simple embedded command.

"Tell me...."

"Tell me..." is a simple two word opening line that simply and naturally invokes the other person to talk and offer up EXACTLY what is on their mind. And it works EVERY single time you use it.

"Tell me...what is the problem?"

"Tell me...what do you think about..."

"Tell me...what is the main issue that you see here?"

"Tell me...more about..."

And my personal favorite: **"Tell me...what are you hearing when I say that?"**

In order for the "Tell me" embedded command to work, it is imperative to be quiet and let the other person speak. A couple of points to remember here:

1. **It does not matter what they say.** So let them say whatever it is they need to. You do not have to like or agree with what they are saying, you just need to *stay curious* throughout the process.

One of my classic stories I like to tell is of a particular social skills session I was facilitating to troubled teens at the Youth Service

Bureau in Slidell, Louisiana. My classes were judge appointed, so I guess you could say most of my students were not exactly clamoring to be in attendance if you catch my meaning. One such attendee was a notably much bigger and stronger seventeen-year-old, who was not wanting to play by the rules of my class and was almost begging to get kicked out. After several minutes of trying to get him to settle down by turning my attention to the other eleven and now on high alert teens in the class, I circled back to him and had the confrontation he wasn't intending.

"James, tell me," I started and then added an emphatic pause, "what is it that you want to do *right now?*"

"You really want to know?" James replied.

"Yes, I'm curious. I really want to know," I offered back.

With just a slight hint of hesitation, but still unfettered, he decreed, "I want to punch you in the face."

"Finally!" I exclaimed, "Now I know where you stand! I stand over here wanting to help you pass my class, and you stand over there wanting to punch me in the face."

I continued on with an exhaling breath of relief, while looking him straight in his eyes, "Now I get it. I feel *much* better, how about you?"

That was a different conversation for James. We had an actual dialogue together—dialogue was not something James was accustomed to having. I gave him room to speak and be heard. Make no mistake, I was completely in control of the conversation, directing every step of the way. The key to my success was in providing a sense of freedom for James which cut right through the stress of the highly intense moment. **I meant business while concurrently giving him the impression he had a choice.** James ended up smiling at me. He ended up getting up and doing the exercise that day. And I am proud to say, James passed my six-week class.

2. **Get curious about what they are saying.**

This is not about waiting to talk. It is about allowing the other side to talk and then connecting with the entry point that you decide

66

on. Listening to their verbiage is key. Using the wording of the other person shows you are listening and unlocks a free flow of information to you (think feelings/assumptions/thoughts etc.). Once you get on *their communication frequency*, they will be open to hearing you.

Check out Stephen Covey's classic book, *The 7 Habits of Highly Successful People*, where he talks about giving people "psychological air." Your level of communication will increase tenfold.

This week, tell me…what are your thoughts on using your "Ninja Style Communication" and where will you start to use it?

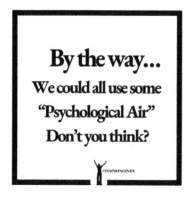

By the way…
We could all use some
"Psychological Air"
Don't you think?

#INSPIRINGINDY

WEEK 20

This Week Rejuvenate from the Mental Body Blow

I got my butt kicked.

I received a real estate text at 7:39a.m. that went like this:

*So have awful news. I had to turn down job. My
wife said she didn't want to move to LA...tried
everything. Waited for her at airport...she wrote me
on plane and said just couldn't make it.
So now not moving. I'm so upset but what can
I do?*

This would have been a sale on a $500,000–$700,000 house. I already spent five hours showing this client properties prior to this trip and spent another two hours doing the prep work of setting up ten more appointments for their next arrival to New Orleans. On top of that, I had another million-dollar deal stall on the negotiation table over an extra $50,000 and a much smaller deal fall apart due to inspections.

That text felt like a body blow to any mental stability I had left. Ever have one of those days?

What do you think my mind was screaming at me inside? Typical responses would seem appropriate—downright necessary, wouldn't you think? That son of a—! Why does this keep happening? I quit! I'm going back to bed!

Not today.

All I heard was "Get dressed!" I immediately put on a Moby playlist on YouTube to get my senses pumping and jumped into the shower. Even my three-year-old daughter knew something was up when she came dancing into my bedroom and asked with delight, "Daddy, where are you going?"

"Honey bear, I'm going for victory today," I proclaimed without hesitation.

Twenty minutes later, after a wonderful Belgian Waffle and coffee breakfast so lovingly conjured up by my amazing wife (she knew I was in a zone), I was out the door.

You see, I was given an opportunity, and I was going to make the most of it. Suddenly I had a very large gap of time to fill, so why not fill it with productivity to get me through the gut-shot I had been delivered? The alternative was to let misery kick in and succumb to the adversity. I could have easily made excuses and who would blame me, right?

Not today.

My very good friend Wisconsin Dave over the years has been a close friend through hard times and victories. We have spent hours on the phone propping each other up through thick and thin. This was a day to put one of his "Dave-isms" to the test—"activity produces activity."

If I get started on an activity, an action step, that will in turn propel me to another activity or step. Sooner or later that activity will build momentum on itself and I will be rejuvenated out of my mental body blow. It works, you just have to be willing to take the first step—any step—which is sometimes the most challenging, am I right?

I did make a quick fifteen-minute call to Wisconsin Dave for a brief rant. "Well this is my 'I just got kicked in the balls voice,' Dave." Cognizant to make sure the call didn't morph into something of a prolonged "Boohooing, woe is me," I buzzed him with the treetop details, listened to his reply and got off the phone.

Then I went to work.

Wouldn't you know immediately upon arriving at the office, I received a lead on a home buyer from my business partner Gregg Tepper and proceeded to get on the hunt for this new client. Immediately after that, I put my head down on a marketing plan to our "Twenty-five Raving Fans" for our real estate team and then put the finishing touches on the first week of the plan with our incredible assistant Joanne.

Now the creative juices were flowing, so I pivoted to writing a script for a new Facebook video that would highlight our team victory of me receiving the local Keller Williams Reality #1 Group Associate of the Year Award. I did a second version tailored to Gregg and a third version for another vendor associate.

Gut-shot? Yes? Down and out?

Not today.

When I arrived home for lunch, I sat down and had a brief and lovely lunch with my wife (it is amazing how arugula, tomatoes, avocadoes, Kalamata olives, and mozzarella cheese with a touch of balsamic vinegar when presented correctly on a plate can be so remarkable to the pallet). Afterwards, I gave her the vision for the Facebook video, and we were off to the races. Within the next two hours, her photography skills and my creativity had storyboarded, shot, and edited the video and had it up and running on Facebook!

Today was not the day to give up. It was the day to take advantage of the gift of adversity. There is a sales class within the Keller Williams ranks called "BOLD" that reminds its participants of one of its "BOLD laws" which seemed appropriate. It proclaims: "You can have excuses or results; you can't have both."

Today, I chose RESULTS.

Take note of the "rejuvenating process."

- Literally get up!
- Put some music on to get the senses kicked in!
- Clean up and get dressed as if you were seeing clients!
- Brief rant/release of negative thoughts—it's okay to get it out!
- Do not, under any circumstances, dwell on the negativity!
- And for crying out loud, show up!
- APA: "Activity produces Activity." So start a positive activity!

This week I will rejuvenate and fight through adversity by:

WEEK 21

This Week Check in with Your Action Accelerator Plan

Yes, that was Week 13. If you have not checked in with your plan, now is the time to do so.

As a reminder, you chose **4 AREAS OF YOUR LIFE** to focus on and then wrote out the three different columns to complete your Action Accelerator Plan.

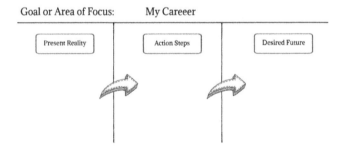

Goal or Area of Focus: My Careeer

Present Reality   Action Steps   Desired Future

What about your **Week 8: Kick-Starter for Life list**? Have you checked in on those ideas and goals?

Now is the time. Don't beat yourself up if you haven't been able to get started on some of them. Yes, sometimes life does get in the way. However, do not make that an excuse. You know where you have been lazy. You know exactly what you need to do in order to achieve some progress.

Here is a keen perspective on taking action from a famous Chinese proverb:

When is the best time to plant a tree?
20 years ago!

When is the next best time?
TODAY!

This week, I will make progress on my Action Accelerator Plan or my Kickstarter for Life Roadmap by:

WEEK 22

Your Week of I Am!

It's time to assert who you are.

It is time to proclaim who you want to be.

It is time to GET INTO YOUR LIFE by DECLARING YOUR POSITIVE AFFIRMATION STATEMENTS!

These affirmation statements are a reminder of who you are in the present tense. They are also an active reminder of who you want to be in the future. These are firm and bold proclamations to anchor you into a daily existence—a personal mission statement, if you will, to maintain a positive focus.

When I look at my declaration, I see a list that says when I daily open the door to participate in the world THIS is how I want to engage it, THIS is how I want to be seen in it. Additionally, each statement breathes into life the essence of the type of impact and energy I want to convey to others—my family, my friends, my colleagues, my clients, and my acquaintances.

Here are my positive affirmation statements that I wrote down in January 2012. I have been grounded in them ever since.

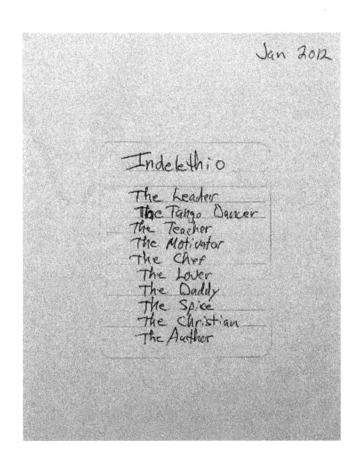

Time to DECLARE who you are and will be for YOUR DAILY IMPACT on the world!
I AM THE…

WEEK 23

The Yes/No Exercise for Your Financial Success!

By now you are hopefully engraining the YES/NO exercise into your daily conscious. So this time around, let's launch into laser focus on growing something important in your life—YOUR FINANCIAL SUCCESS.

From my real estate experience, I have listened to countless stories of people being afraid of knowing, or better, UNDERSTANDING their financial position and therefore stay frozen into non-action which then propels them deeper into financial despair. This "non-action" translates into NO PLAN for the future. Their assumption is that the financial problem is SO BIG that it is an impossible abyss to navigate, so rather than face the situation head on, they hide—hide from reality. Hide from help. Hide from starting on the road to success.

Hear now from Stephanie Weeks of The Weeks Team Mortgage in Covington, Louisiana, whom I affectionately call the "Lending Lady" on why it is so important to face debt and your financial plan head on:

> Let's face it and be direct and serious...looking at your debt sucks and can be overwhelming. Heck, even embarrassing!
>
> It's so exciting to look at a house and to think about plans and goals. However, it's not exciting to come face-to-face and talk head-to-head with a lender so that they can talk you through this process. It appears to be a very scary thing, but honestly, it's not. It really ISN'T.
>
> It's a matter of starting with one simple phone call where you say:
>
> "I want to buy a house in (this time frame)."
>
> "I want to come up with (this much money) to buy a house."
>
> "I want a payment of (this much)."
>
> "Am I there? Could I be approved? And if I'm not, how do I get there?"
>
> It as simple as picking up the phone and dialing and starting with that little bit of information. That's it! No scary monster jumping out from the dark!
>
> The lender can then guide you, step by step, on how to get from *A* to *Z*. It's not as horrible

as people think. Sometimes people think they're a year out when they're really just a month out. You never know unless you simply make that first phone call.

(Stephanie Weeks "The Lending Lady" of The Weeks Team Lending in Covington, LA)

And also, from Jack Branch, financial advisor of Branch Wealth Strategies on the importance of not being in the dark with debt and your financial plan:

If what you thought was true about your wealth turned out to be untrue, when would you want to know?

I have spent nearly two decades watching people live their lives in a mindset of being "customers of the bank"—in debt, out of control, and their finances like a junk drawer in your kitchen. My job is to teach those that want more for their life, to shift their mindset to one of living like they are "The Bank."

It saddens me that many people are house rich but cash poor, 401K rich but liquidity poor, or are trying to impress people with their toys vs. their financial literacy. A mentor of mine once told me, "A pay raise only becomes effective once *you* become effective! Maybe it's time to step into the light with your financial plan?"

(Jack Branch, Branch Wealth Strategies)

When it comes to your FINANCIAL SUCCESS...
What will you say YES to?
What will you say NO to?

This week I will say YES to...
and therefore, I will say NO to...

This week I will say NO to...
and therefore, I will say YES to...

Or you can make YES/NO affirmation statements for your week:
This week I say YES to...
This week I say NO to...

Remember to use
YES/NO as your filter
in order to make your
decisions that much
more impactful!

#INSPIRINGINDY

WEEK 24

This Week Take the Extraordinary Step to Becoming a Profound Leader

Learn how to follow.

A beautiful concept that I extracted from tango and implemented into my executive coaching is the following:

"The leader must consider the follower in order to truly make the dance work" **(unknown).**

And therefore, as a leader, I have come to understand:

If I understand the fears of the follower, I can speak to them more acutely.

And if I speak to them more acutely, I will truly know how they listen.

If I know how they listen, I will be able to move them to hear me more deeply.

And if they hear me more deeply, I will open up their vulnerability.

If I grasp their vulnerability, I can illuminate a path for their trust.

And if I access their trust, I can motivate them with a synergistic energy, intuitively moving us together as one, rather than struggling against a wall of negativity.

How can you get here?

Put on the shoes of a follower. Listen as a follower. Allow the leader to lead while actively aware of the wake they leave for you to walk through. Be on alert, you will have the potential to either learn behavior to exemplify down the road or absorb a list of what not to do when you are in charge. Do not miss this opportunity. Remember, this is training for when you are leading the way.

Take your following seriously.

Profound leadership results await you once you take this extraordinary step.

"He who cannot be a good follower cannot be a good leader" **(Aristotle).**

Pro Tip: This also works in personal relationships.

List here ALL of the people that you follow:

This week I will take the extraordinary step of following in order to become a profound leader by:

In Order to Transfer
Extraodinary
Leadership...

Learn How to
Follow Well.

@INSPIRINGINDY

WEEK 25

This Week Check Your Level of Leadership

By asking yourself, **WHO FOLLOWS ME?**

In his famous leadership book, *Develop the Leader Within You*, John Maxwell lays out his "levels of leadership" as the foundation of the leadership landscape. The bottom level or first level that he lays out is leading from "position" or "title" only. Maxwell explains that if one leads from this level, people only follow you because they have to. You can imagine how motivated people are if they are only responding to the title and not the actual person. Once the leader is out of sight, the desire of the follower falls off dramatically.

You do not want to be at this level, at least, not for a very long period of time.

Let's take the question one step further.

WHO DO YOU INFLUENCE?

This question aims at the heart of what leadership truly is—influence.

I once worked with a leadership coaching client who at first blush told me that they did not lead anyone. This stemmed from their "official" title. When I presented the "influence" question to them, the light bulb turned on. Turns out this client of mine, when they did the actual investigation, discovered that not only did they have people who they influenced, they actually had multiple groups—PLURAL—that they influenced! This newfound perspective empowered my client to go from being told by a superior that they were a "wallflower" to "You are a BUILDER" all within a year's timeframe. Once they figured out that they did not need a certain title to lead change, they were off to the races. The result? A complete system change of the department due to their leading—influencing—of people.

These are the questions to consider:

- Who follows me?
- Who do I influence?
- Who must follow me?
- Who wants to follow me?
- Who do I want to follow me?

You may consider yourself a "leader;" however, when you look back behind you, are there people actually following?

If yes, why?

If no, why not?

With any of these questions, if you want to improve, you must figure out the "INFLUENCE" dynamic to increase your leadership productivity. Ultimately, the true test of your leadership is if people still want to follow even when there is no directive to do so. This applies not only in the workplace but also with your clients, customers, and personal relationships. If I am truly contributing to the relationship, whatever that may be, I will usually shine in the process.

This week I will investigate the "influence" question in my life by:

When people
come into contact
with you...
What is the IMPACT
of your
PRESENCE?

#INSPIRINGINDY

WEEK 26

This Week You Are the Star!

There are people in the world, in your community, and in your family that **NEED TO EXPERIENCE YOU!**

The question is, are you worth being experienced in your current state?

Let's be honest, if we have any self-awareness about ourselves at all, we would conclude there are areas of our life that could be upgraded, retouched, or even overhauled.

Over the years I have asked this question not only of my coaching clients but of myself as well.

Would you hire you right now?

Would you date you right now?

Would you buy you right now?

Would you follow you right now?

NOW IS THE TIME TO GO AND BECOME INTERESTING.

Now, do not get my meaning wrong. This is not about being obnoxious and seeking attention. I love the quote from the movie *The Secret Life of Walter Mitty*, which reminds us that "[b]eautiful things don't need to be told they're beautiful." Or the German proverb, "Glory seeks those who flee it and flees those who chase it."

I find it interesting that we as a society demand only the best for ourselves, but what about *demanding the best* **from** *ourselves*?

Here's the thing about becoming interesting—you become *interested*. Interested in a hobby, a group, the other person, a technique, an idea, etc. Take the focus off of being "seen" to one of seeing and experiencing.

By collecting experiences, you will accumulate a treasure full of knowledge and stories to share which is very attractive!

This brings us full circle.

You need to experience people, and people need to experience you. Remember your "Inner Energizing Honey Bee" from Week 4? You may not be in your "ideal" state right now, and that is okay, you just need to get started—APA, ACTIVITY PRODUCES ACTIVITY (hint: it is a good idea to always be in a growth mindset rather than one of stagnation).

Or you may feel absolutely ecstatic about yourself, then go spread the wealth, friend, and make a positive difference (hint: self-absorption is not attractive and leads to emptiness inside).

Again, this does not have to be complicated. Keep it simple. Start with your family and friends; there is always opportunity to "freshen up" these relationships. Or be adventurous and get on the radar of someone that does not know you and see what possibilities are there for both their growth and yours. And when you start to seek out experiences, think active engagement.

So put down the gadget, get away from the computer, and stop watching the TV! I once showed a real estate client a very beautiful and expensive house, but they complained about it because "it did not have a perfect place for the TV." In fact, there was only one TV in the entire home, the rest of the walls and rooms were covered with various pieces of artwork. The current owner WAS the artist! It was wonderfully obvious that this owner was actively engaged in becoming interesting.

This week I will start becoming interesting by:

"My life is like a Grand Piano; I'm always seeking ways to use all of my keys to make incredible music!" -Inspiring Indy

Scoreboard

This is your 2nd Quarter Check-up. How are you doing so far with each exercise?

- ☐ Week 14: Smell the Flowers and Blow Out the Candles
- ☐ Week 15: Fill Emotional Piggy Bank
- ☐ Week 16: 30 Minutes of Self-Care: Tell Your Body I Love You
- ☐ Week 17: Creative Master Through Chaos
- ☐ Week 18: A Letter to Some One Who Needs to Hear from You
- ☐ Week 19: Ninja Style Communication
- ☐ Week 20: Rejuvenate from the Mental Body Blow
- ☐ Week 21: Action Accelerator Plan
- ☐ Week 22: The Week of I Am
- ☐ Week 23: Yes/No Exercise to Financial Success
- ☐ Week 24: Your Step to Being a Profound Leader
- ☐ Week 25: Check Your Level of Leadership
- ☐ Week 26: This Week You Are the Star

WEEK 27

30 Minutes of Self-Care This Week

It's that time again to take a moment to focus on loving yourself.

Again, as a reminder, fifteen years of coaching individuals, this is one of the BIGGEST challenges I have listened to from people on all levels—taking time to take care of ourselves.

Hear from Shawn Blair on how she is 100 percent engaged in transforming people's mindset of loving their bodies in a way that impacts their health through her Nutrition Revolution:

> For the past nine and a half years, I've kept my clients engaged by building genuine, relationships. I honestly feel like in order to help anyone achieve results and transform their mental and physical state you have to know and understand their goals and their WHY! WHY do they want to achieve these results? WHY now? What makes this time different? It is also important to have realistic expectations and realize that no one gains a hundred pounds in three months and therefore you can't expect to lose it in that same timeframe.
>
> Keeping things simple and celebrating milestones throughout the journey is paramount. The process of transformation isn't about MAJOR changes, it's about simple changes compounded day after day and having someone to support this journey is extremely important.

(Shawn Blair, Nutrition Revolution)

What is one personal attribute or milestone you will celebrate this week?

Say this out loud
with me...

It is OK
To Take Care of Myself.

WEEK 28

Catapult Yourself Out of the Rut

Experience something NEW!

This really is a challenge to you this week—a challenge with a deeper engagement if you choose to accept.

I want you to go experience something NEW AND LET YOURSELF BE A BEGINNER!

Yes, this will make you feel vulnerable.

Yes, this will make you uncomfortable (at first).

This is where you get to tap back into your beautiful three-year-old curiosity again. Remember that person? Don't you wish that you could? I witnessed it in my three older boys when they were younger. Today I actively engage in this enchantment on a daily basis with my three-year-old daughter and five-year-old son.

Daddy, what does this do?

Mommy, why does that go that way?

Daddy, can you show me how this works?

Mommy, let me try!

Daddy, I can do it!

Beginners. Curious.

Willing to try.

Looking through the lens of possibility.

No concept of failure.

Over the years, I have tried many new things. I have moved to various new states, and by virtue of location, I had to engage my new surroundings in order to survive. As I look back, I noticed that my personality, while drawn to the experience of exploring and meeting people, had a tendency to not always enter situations completely open and probably in many cases, closed up. Maybe it's the guy in me that needed to show off that I knew what I was doing, not wanting to come across as stupid. Maybe it was a maturing process I needed to work through. Whatever it was, I saw it as a blind spot in my life, and I was bound to change it.

My mechanism? Argentine tango.

I equate Argentine tango as the tai-chi of dance. It has many steps and combinations, however, not one dance or *tanda,* as it is called, is the same. It has a certain flow and yet allows for artistic freedom. There is no going on auto-pilot as each partner must "listen" to each other's embrace. Argentine tango is like playing chess while all other dances are like playing checkers.

It is an intoxicating proficiency.

Tango is part of me. I wake up and I sleep with it every day...
I fell in love with tango and changed all my life for it. I think that the secret of tango is that it takes everyone, touches everyone and puts everyone together... It's real, it's sharing, it's giving and receiving, it's also communicating with people that sometimes don't even speak your language!
Tango is universal. Dancing is a therapy and we all need it! It makes you feel good and beautiful. When I dance tango, I express myself, I live a story with each and every one I embrace. I give a part of me and he gives me his...that creates "our" tango. Each one has something to tell, a story to share. For me tango is: Emotion. You can be happy, sad, surprised, angry...It's a constant Motivation that makes you always want more!

(Pam Est Là, Direzione Artistica of Dos Corazones Tango Accademia, Rimini, Italy)

Opening the floodgates even more, once a working level of ability is achieved, Argentine tango is a universal language that can be expressed with people from all over the globe.
Pretty intense place of "new," wouldn't you say?
It is.
It's also extremely difficult.
And intimidating.
This is the arena in which I decided to be a beginner. And for three years I was smitten. I took classes. I watched videos. I practiced my "tango walk" daily. I had tango music playing wherever I went, even to the extent of playing it while I slept. I asked questions. I let the teachers be the expert. **And I allowed myself to "mess up."**

After about a year, I found other people asking *me* questions. I became so enamored with the dance that I became an ambassador for tango by starting my own little class for beginners. By allowing myself to be a beginner, I opened the door to deeper learning and understanding. I didn't "skip steps" because of my pride or ego which in turn made me excel even further. You know you have arrived when women start approaching you out of nowhere to say, "Please save a dance for me."

Fully accepting the beginner mode also gave me an appreciation for other new dancers that would come to milongas or classes I was participating in and most certainly for the ones I was facilitating. I knew what those "first night jitters" felt like (it took me twenty minutes of sitting outside the dance studio in my truck before I went into my first class). I understood how welcoming a calm, friendly hand was while fighting through frustration of forgetting steps or awkwardly trying them out for the first time. And I uncovered a new level of confidence that I didn't know I had been cowering inside for years—what a gift!

Looking back in my mental rearview mirror, I am able to see that I touched all of the steps in the journey. For once, I didn't leap over any of the stages because of my feeling insecure. This, ironically, gave me some inner peace and an ability to have an eye on the horizon of continual learning ahead. I finally achieved the level of understanding that I craved.

Start Here

No one is going to knock on your door to motivate you.

No one is going to call you out-of-the-blue and say, "Hey, it's time to start believing in yourself."

You must find it inside of yourself and say, "Today is my day!"

If you do not believe in yourself, why should anyone else?

It is time to start believing in YOU.

During my acting phase in New York City, I also became a beginner and started painting pictures. I was just drawn to the creative process and the ability to let my imagination run wild. It was also a way of celebrating myself. I enjoyed the satisfaction of completing a vision I had in my mind and capturing it on paper or canvass. And it created an atmosphere of believing in myself. Living in a gigantic place like New York City, where it is easy to get swallowed up into obscurity by the mass of people fighting to be #1, I had to start at home with my belief that I deserve to be in the game!

So I started hanging my pictures on my apartment walls. And I loved it. All of my creations came to life in front of me each and every day—it was a celebration of my creativity.

Then one day I was tested.

An actor acquaintance dropped by my place to say HI and hang out for a bit. When he walked into the living room and saw my pieces on the wall, he blurted out with a certain distain, "You actually hang them on the wall!?" It was like he was telling me, "How dare you have the audacity to show yourself off."

It was my moment to either wither in embarrassment or indeed, believe in myself.

I proclaimed back, "Yes, I love them! It's my art."

A couple of weeks later, my upstairs neighbor came down to tell me that they were leaving the area and wanted to say goodbye. When she saw my art on my living room walls, she would not stop gushing about my "Elegant Green Lady." She loved it so much she asked if she could buy it from me. I sold it to her for $25!

So now it is your turn. It is time to get out of the rut. Allow yourself to be a BEGINNER. Allow yourself to TRY SOMETHING NEW. Allow yourself to BELIEVE IN YOU.

Where will you start? What will your "Argentine tango" be? What will your "painting" be??

Movie inspiration: *Joe versus The Volcano* with Tom Hanks and *The Secret Life of Walter Mitty* with Ben Stiller.

This week I will try something new and engage being a beginner by:

WEEK 29

This Week Invest in Someone's Life

I bought bees.

I have always had an affinity toward bees (yes, see Week 4 again for a reminder). They are truly one of God's remarkable creations. How well they work together in harmony with one goal in mind is incredibly fascinating. And the bee's impact on the word? Utterly and shockingly astonishing.

That all being said, I will probably never have a bee farm. It's just not in the cards for me. Having the proper amount of space, tools, knowhow, and true desire to put in the time and effort is just not there for me. This, however, does not mean I cannot live vicariously through someone else and support their effort.

Enter Gary.

Gary is a survivalist. He is currently working on making his Bar M Homestead come alive and self-sustaining. And I am a tiny part of it.

Over the past three or four years, we were trying to find just the right property for his budget, and once we did, we got it under contract. After the sales date, I told Gary I wanted to be a part of his process and help out again where I could—I even hinted at helping him with bees. He did the polite thing and nodded but didn't take me seriously.

About six months later, I saw Gary at the Act Hardware store he manages and asked about how the bees were coming along. He told me he had been trying everything the members of the bee group at the local farmer's market had suggested but was not able to coax any colonies into his boxes.

"Gary, I told you I wanted to help. How much do the bees cost?" I asked directly with a smile.

Without a pause he offered back, "$125."

"I'll be right back," I said, and went straight to my truck. When I came back, I handed Gary a check. "Go buy some bees."

"Thanks!" he said with a big smile. "I'll get on it tomorrow."

About three months later, wouldn't you know it, Gary presented me with eight beautiful jars of local honey. And for some strange reason, maybe it is because I had a part in it, that honey is by far the best honey I have ever tasted.

I also follow the updates on Gary's Bar M Homestead Facebook page with a certain pride knowing I was and am a part of that story and journey. All for $125. The only strings attached are my curiosity about what is next for the Homestead and when's the next batch of honey arriving.

Someone is out there that could use your support. Not your advice or opinion, your support—be it monetary or a helping hand. Go seek this out. Everyone wins and you will be so much the better for it.

Side note: Please, for goodness sake, do not get hung up on the $125! You know exactly how much to offer. Whatever your "$125" is will be the correct amount.

This week I will invest in someone else by:

WEEK 30

I'm Back!

This week, check in with your Action Accelerator Plan.

Yes, that was Week 13 and again in Week 21.

If you have not checked in with your plan, now is the time to do so.

Goal or Area of Focus: My Careeer

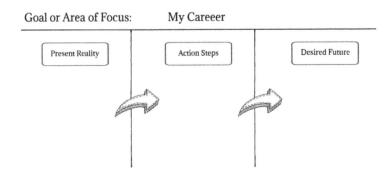

As a reminder, you chose **4 AREAS OF YOUR LIFE** to focus on and then wrote out the three different columns to complete your Action Accelerator Plan.

What about your **Week 8 Kick-Starter for Life List**??? Have you checked in on those ideas and goals?

Now is the time. Don't beat yourself up if you haven't been able to get started on some of them. Yes, sometimes life does get in the way. However, do not make that an excuse. You know where you have been lazy. You know exactly what you need to do in order to achieve some progress.

From Giovanni Livera's Book, *Live a Thousand Years,* I give you his question:

? - ?

If your gravestone had these three pieces of information on it:

- a question mark for when you were *born*
- a dash for when you *lived*
- and a question mark for when you *die*

What would be the most important piece of information on the gravestone?

If you answered "the dash," you are correct! That is where you live, where you make your mark, where you deliver an impact!

From this perspective, isn't it time to live your life a bit differently?

This week I will be intentional in my life by:

The Question is:

Are you letting
THE
SABOTAGE
VOICE
win?

WEEK 31

Your "Yeah? Watch Me!" Triumph

Weeks heading into my flight to go the Philippines for the first time to meet my "possible future wife," people came out of the woodwork, it seemed, to give me their opinion on what they thought about my trip. I heard a lot of "I could never do that" and many versions of "What ifs"—"What if this happens?" and "What if that happens?"

The short version of the story is that as a part of the social skills program for troubled youth that I created and facilitated, I also did a side class for kids who got in trouble on the internet. To stay ahead of the game and understand these kids better, I went looking for trouble on the internet as well. As a result, I became very good at learning and identifying how individuals work to scam innocent people. Soon my personal interests intertwined with my work motivation, and I found myself on the international Craigslist pages.

For about two months, I was engaged in a back-and-forth with someone who was definitely trying to "catfish" me—that is, keep telling me a story to get me hooked, fall in love, continually ask for money but then never show up.

I was given names of the hospitals in my area that they were supposedly interviewing with. I was even given a plane itinerary when they were going to arrive. And yes, I sent them some money.

They never showed up.

I finally figured out that the "catfish" person was using some-one else's identity. When I discovered the true identity of the pictures, I notified this person immediately with a couple of messages on Facebook.

Three months later, out of the blue, the real person responded.

That initial conversation and the next subsequent five months with many, many hours of texting and Skyping went from a "Thank you for the heads' up" to curiosity and friendship which blossomed into "Wait, this might be the one!" Call it intuition, I just had a "feeling" this could be something special. And the rest, as they say, is history. As of this writing, Anya and I will have been married for almost five years and have two beautiful children. She is the most incredible person that I know.

We truly are a match made in heaven.

This trip was not a whim. It was something I thought and prayed about night and day. I did not take it lightly. It was also, regardless of the outcome, an incredibly HUGE moment in my life. Let me repeat that, MY LIFE. For the first time ever, I was traveling by myself to the other side of the world. Up to this point, I had always had a companion wherever I went. This time I was finally taking the call on my own.

Personally, it was a breakthrough. It was the sidebar story no one knew about or would understand anyway. Just like when I changed my name at age twenty to my great-great-great grandfather's name—Indelethio—it was my "Yeah? Watch Me!" Triumph that made a deep, indelible, life-changing impact on my existence.

One little extra detail I want to include about this time is this quote I would see every morning at the Keller Williams office. It read: **"A great pleasure in life is doing what people say you cannot do."**

I smile every time I think about the days leading up to my trip and reading this. I hope that it is a motivating reminder for you as well.

Another person I know who has experience with a "Yeah? Watch Me!" moment in her life is Ioana Garrett, business and marketing strategist and executive producer and show host of *Success Stalkers*. Take note as she shares an encounter with her own "Yeah? Watch Me!" Triumph and displays how it can be the one action that propels you to the success you have been seeking,

> ### Are you prepared to go through
> # The Tunnel of the Unknown
> #### in order to meet what awaits you on the other side?
> #INSPIRINGINDY

It was in 2009 when the idea that I could start a movement of people who were relentless and unapologetic for going after their success. People who were so passionate and so relentless, that it almost seemed like they were stalking it. Hence the name "Success Stalkers" was born. I can remember when I shared the idea with someone whom I once respected very deeply. He laughed and thought it was a silly idea and I was CRUSHED. That's when I had my "Yeah? Watch me!" triumph! I simply refused to allow what he said to put my fire out. I knew there were successful people out there, and I also knew there were people out there who were hungry to find out how to become successful. So, I decided to interview both of these types of people in the form of a podcast. Little did I know it would become so popular and I would become the host of a GLOBAL podcast show. We now have over forty thousand listeners in over eighty-three countries!

(Ioana Garrett, *Success Stalkers*)

Your "Yeah? Watch Me!" Triumph is waiting for you.

Please note: This is not a spur of the moment action. This is an action that needs to be slept on for a period of time but one that more than likely needs to take place in order for you to "breakthrough." Seek wisdom throughout the process.

The "Yeah? Watch Me" Triumph makes me think about… (start writing)

Question...

Whose life is it?
That's right,
it's your life!

 #INSPIRINGINDY

WEEK 32

It's Awards Week!

This week I want you to hand-pick a person or a couple of people to
AWARD with CELEBRATION!

Think of it as a creative way to say, "Thank you for being in
my life." It is a way of showing gratitude. And it is a way of exalting

someone else for no other reason than to express how much you care about them. So turn the spotlight off of yourself this week and direct it onto a special handpicked person and enjoy the dividends that it pays for both you and the highlighted individual.

Years ago, I made "Golden Whistle Awards" and presented one to each one of my clients in front of my business networking group. I've been told years later how some of those same people have the whistles still hanging in their offices.

My real estate partner and I have come up with our "Raving Fans" group and set in place a plan for reaching out to them to show our gratitude and touching them throughout the year.

And occasionally I have been known to declare a special day to a friend or colleague by using their name and calling them to announce, "It's Will Cullen Appreciation Day" as an example. This would then be followed up with a full course meal of pepper-corned filet mignon grilled to perfection, topped with a shallot-balsamic-infused blue cheese melting all over it, garlic mashed potatoes, and a side arugula salad with apple slices, more blue cheese crumbles, drizzled with olive oil, and a dusting of salt and black pepper, all prepared by yours truly. Of course, this is all paired with the wine or beer of their choosing and finished off with a homemade dessert from my wife. Then we adjourn to some darts and billiards with some fantastic music, and you have yourself a pretty well played out "appreciation day."

There was one time one of my "Appreciation Day" friends exclaimed to me that he had never been treated so well in all his life. Going out of your way to make someone feel special "out of the blue" and celebrating them without need of reciprocation can feel incredibly well inside.

Need extra incentive? Re-read Week 5: Find Your Inner Oasis Superpowers.

So WHO DO YOU WANT TO CELEBRATE?

My highlighted handpicked list of people I want to celebrate is:

WEEK 33

This Week I Have a Big Question for You

Are you **the HERO** or **the TRUSTED GUIDE?**

In his mind-shifting book, *Building a Storybrand,* author Donald Miller poses this question as his platform for creating a marketing story that makes truly lasting impact on customers, clients, and even workgroups within businesses. I find it a uniquely posited question and one that evokes certain actions depending on the perspective chosen.

Are you the HERO running around in your story, trying to save the day with all of its ups, downs, and obstacles, or are you the TRUSTED GUIDE offering up solutions and the direction needed to the path of victory?

Interestingly, each have their own glory; however, isn't the HERO what you gravitated toward the most? For some reason, doesn't the HERO seem more exciting? Doesn't your ego want you to be seen as the one "saving the day"? And maybe you are. Maybe you are the one "breaking down walls" and "rescuing" the people around you because in the end, isn't this what a leader does?

Let me present to you a mental shift.

As a leader, you may feel or think you are acting as the hero, but in fact, I will challenge you to see for your leadership growth and understanding, you need to see yourself as the TRUSTED GUIDE. As Donald Miller points out:

The day we stop losing sleep over the success of our business and start losing sleep over the success of our customers is the day our business will start growing again. (*Building a Storybrand*, p.77)

Now exchange the word business with the word leadership and the word customers with the words *people we lead*, and you may see a new reality:

The day we stop losing sleep over the success of our *leadership* and start losing sleep over the success of *the people we lead* is the day our *leadership* will start growing again.

In your leadership, if you start seeing the people you lead as the hero, your impact will undoubtedly increase with a depth your first-person voice could only begin to dream of. And of course, your role as leader can come in many different facets—because of your title in an organization, because of your knowledge in a certain genre, or because particular people in your sphere of influence actually NEED YOUR DIRECTING. You are the TRUSTED GUIDE for these people.

In a truly inspiring example, I had a leadership client who was having difficulty connecting with their boss, so much so, they had lost all desire to even want to work with them on any issues at work. However, they were forced to the reality that they needed to eventually get "the boss" on board with their idea for change and therefore needed to engage with them. I presented to my leadership client the idea of making *the boss the hero* in the story.

Of course, at first, this did not make any sense to my client because "they (the boss) are a complete jerk and are afraid to lead. Why should they be the hero?" I went on to point out that my leadership client needed to position themselves as the TRUSTED GUIDE, even to "the boss," and eventually, they, my leadership client, would start to see the winds of change. In fact, this is exactly what happened. "The boss" was truly at a loss when it came to having answers or solutions and was indeed hiding from the department. When my leadership client started acting as the TRUSTED GUIDE and at the same time seeing "the boss" as the HERO, suddenly "the boss" welcomed my client because they were helping SOLVE THEIR PROBLEM. And by being seen as the SOLUTION, my client started being recognized as THE LEADER. This was shockingly acknowledged when "the boss" told my client, "One day you will take over my position."

By taking my coaching, my leadership client started to appeal to the first-person hero voice of "the boss"—their need and desire to win and get on the road to victory.

Hear now from Pastor Aaron Robinson, a pastor, who for the past nineteen years has been a TRUSTED GUIDED in New York City to Milwaukee, Wisconsin to even Lusaka, Zambia.

> Recently, I had the opportunity to be a part of the same Little League program that I played in as a child. This time as a coach to my son, as my dad had been a coach to me. On the first week back as

I assisted with my youngest son's team, I couldn't believe what I saw. I saw my old coach. He was still at the ballpark. Throughout the summer I had more of those experiences and I began to appreciate what these men meant in my life. I recognize that throughout my life from teachers to pastors, coaches to neighbors I have been guided by men and women that were in my life. They showed me a path, they guided me as best they could.

Having a "trusted guide" is important for everyone. It is so important that it is a trope in epic stories and classic movies. Where would Luke have been if he didn't have old Ben Kenobi? How far would Frodo have gotten without Sam? Could John Snow have survived the White Walkers without Davos? In all of these stories, the "trusted guide" is just as important to a successful outcome as the hero.

There are three things that a "trusted guide" does. First, they understand their role. In my role as a shepherd of God's flock I get the privilege of pointing people to Jesus, the ultimate hero AND trusted guide. He in reality did more than Luke, John Snow or Frodo did in fiction. Secondly, the "trusted guide" seeks to build relationships with people so that there is a bond of trust. Trust, not borne out of thinking you have all the answers, rather, trust in the understanding that your leadership is not out of self-interest. And lastly, the "trusted guide" is okay with saying, "I don't know, let's go on this journey together."

May you be a blessing to others as a "trusted guide" and may the "trusted guides" in your life be plentiful.

(Pastor Aaron Robinson)

This week examine your various roles and see how the TRUSTED GUIDE PERSPECTIVE can influence the way you operate. Remember, when you help your HEROES win, YOU WIN.

Consider your roles:

- with coworkers
- with clients and customers
- with your spouse or significant other
- with your children
- with your friends and acquaintances

Write down who your possible "HEROES" are and how you can help them WIN:

> When Helping Your
> "Heroes"
> Ponder the use of:
>
> **"It appears for your victory in this matter, you may want to consider..."**
>
> INSPIRINGINDY

WEEK 34

This Week Be the Person Who Creates Magic

Every year to celebrate Easter, my family does two important things—first, we go to church to celebrate the resurrection of Jesus, and second, we eat crawfish.

Now while it's no secret that eating crawfish in Louisiana is a ceremony in itself, at my house, on Easter, it's a happening! Why? Because I intentionally put "magic" into the event to make it special for the day itself and a lasting memory for years to come for my family.

The "magic" starts right out of the gate as I employ my younger kids to wash the crawfish. I let them know this is a very important job (and it is. Who wants gritty crawfish?) and it usually takes a good four to five rinses to get the job done. The kids love it. They feel a part of the process, and besides, what child doesn't love playing with the water hose?

Next comes the preparation for the crawfish Easter toast. Everyone in my family knows what this means. "Dad, are we having the Crawfish Cooler this year?" Or even better, "Dad, can I help make the Crawfish Cooler this year?" This is another added element to the "magic." Simply labeling the drink and making it a part of the celebration brings the moment to life for everyone involved. Tell me, which would you rather drink, Blue Hawaiian Punch Kool-Aid with orange juice and Sprite or the "Crawfish Cooler"? Topping the drink off with even more "magic" are premade "crawfish ice cubes" consisting of orange juice and one whole raspberry for each cube. We even have special cups to drink out of. All part of the "magic."

Next in line are the "crawfish races" with everyone in attendance, picking out their preferred, live crawfish to "race" off of their individual square on the patio. The winners of the all three heats then compete in one last race for the prize of being the "crawfish paddle winner"!

And then it's time to feast!

Ceremony. Tradition. Magic.

I became keenly aware of this nuance as a teenager when I became interested in cooking various classic traditional menu offerings. One such item was the "baked Alaska." Baked Alaska? What is this? And look how interesting and rich it looked! However, the adults around me completely deflated my intrigue by offering their disclaimer of "Oh, that's just cake and ice cream."

"Oh, that's just…" It is the "magic" destroyer.

I finally was able to get "Wisconsin Dave" to see the light on offering the "magic" as well. He and I have a very different view of food. I see food as an experience, and he sees it as a means to an end. That being said, Wisconsin Dave, along with his wife, are very social people and are either consistently going to a gathering or having one at their home throughout the year. And with any gathering comes food. So I prodded Dave to come up with a dish of his own. "Dave, with as many parties that you have or go to, you really should have a dish you are known for!" (magic). Of course, understanding that he can't (or won't) boil water, I knew this would be a tall order. One day I found a fantastically delicious AND easy to make New Orleans BBQ shrimp recipe and emailed it over.

After about three or four parties, they have now become "Dave's Shrimp."

Magic!

So, the question is this:

Are you going to be the person that says, **"Oh, that's just…"** or are you going to be the person **"adding the magic"?**

This week I will create "MAGIC" by:

WEEK 35

This Week Play Like a Champion

Exude the Dr. Bobby Rodwig "Climbing the Ladder to Success" plan.

Champions play on a different level than most. Champions are persistent. They are the ones grinding it out while other have called it quits. Champions know that talent only goes so far, so they put in the hard work of growing their knowledge and skill level. Champions find the path to YES rather than being the wedge of negativity. And yes, champions have longevity because they consistently win—defeat is just a speed bump to success, it does not define who they are.

Enter Dr. Bobby Rodwig.

Dr. Rodwig has been a leadership client of my mine for many years, but in reality, we are colleagues. We have learned from and helped each other mutually, and I am truly thankful and inspired to be a part of his journey.

I met Dr. Rodwig just on the heels of him being thrust into the pathology chairman role, as well as being the head of the blood bank for Ochsner Hospital in New Orleans, Louisiana. Additionally, added to his "large shoes to fill" position was the aftermath of Hurricane Katrina that threw the entire city into physical and emotional havoc. However, this former Tulane football quarterback had the pedigree of grit, finesse, and "team mentality" to lead his area of the hospital through such a devastating period.

Fast forward to the present, over a career that has spanned twenty-seven years and counting, you get to witness a champion at the "top of their game" as they say. But how does one go from a seemingly just everyday pathologist to chairperson to lead physician liaison as the professional services medical director for the entire Ochsner Medical System in the Gulf South?

By being a champion.

Hear now from Dr. Rodwig on his "Steps of Climbing the Ladder to Success" that I have captured over the years:

"Show up!"

So many people hide—don't be one of those people. By actually being present, you are already ahead of many people because they could not make the effort.

"Make yourself AVAILABLE"

By making yourself AVAILABLE, you are saying I am a willing part of the team which makes you very approachable and likely to be tapped for a bigger role down the road.

"Make yourself INVALUABLE"

When you are the person whose default is, "YES, I CAN GET THAT DONE!" and you follow through, you become INVALUABLE to any team. This translates into you eventually becoming the "go-to authority."

"Again, SHOW UP!"

I cannot stress this enough. So many people don't or won't.

"VOLUNTEER for something"

When you want to become seen and known, this is the place to start. Additionally, you will always draw from these experiences throughout your career.

"DO NOT Complain"

Not ever! Once you start complaining, you are the road to losing. Not to mention your reputation as a "complainer" will precede you wherever you go.

"Attack the PREPARATION"

Read, read, and read some more. Your arsenal of knowledge can never be too big. When it comes time for that big, important meeting or presentation, you will shine the brightest in the room because you were the most prepared.

"Intentionally recognize with GRATITUDE"

- Send handwritten thank-you notes while being specific in the message: "Thank you for…"
- Email your boss to praise an employee and cc: that employee.
- Pay small compliments in front of others—this increases the likelihood of chime-in from the group,

- Train mentors to recognize effort—they often see what we don't.
- Acknowledge someone's absence—let them know they were missed because they are valued!

This week I will PLAY LIKE A CHAMPION!

I will SHOW UP BY...

I will make myself AVAILABLE **for...**

I will make myself INVALUABLE **to...**

I will VOLUNTEER **for...**

When I hear COMPLAINING, **I will...**

I will ATTACK MY PREPARATION **by...**

I will RECOGNIZE OTHERS WITH GRATITUDE **by...**

WEEK 36

The Yes/No Exercise with Accountability

This week, I am challenging you to do your YES/NO exercise with an accountability partner!

I am here to remind you, do not go it alone. Get someone involved in your process in order to break through to the next level of your success. Whatever your ambition, if you want to set yourself apart from the crowd, get yourself an accountability partner. Maybe it is a trusted friend or maybe it is a professional that you hire—whomever it is, now is the time to find that person in your life.

Hear now from Celeste Marcussen Hart, owner of the modeling and talent agency, Creating U, on the importance of having accountability for success.

> As the owner of Creating U, an Acting, Modeling and Life Etiquette Academy, I have positioned myself as a partner to my students. Focusing on the Acting aspect, in order for my students to be successful, I keep them accountable to attend every class prepared, take yearly professional headshots and attend/tape every audition they receive. They are required to be memorized on their scenes, rehearsed, have had good sleep and are hair/makeup ready. On the flip side, as their partner, I provide excellent Coaching—which means keeping up with all present acting techniques, provide a topnotch photographer and am rested with high energy to help them reach their goals. For our success together, accountability is a must because a standard is set for both sides of the partnership. Those students that shy away from this process only flounder in the end...I see that time and time again.

> **(CelesteMarcussen Hart, Creating U Acting & Modeling Agency)**

The person(s) I will invite to be my YES/NO partner is/are:

It is Impossible
to See
"Blind Spots"
by
Yourself.

#INSPIRINGINDY

How is the YES/NO exercise showing up in your daily routine?

This week I will say YES to...

and therefore, I will say NO to...

This week I will say NO to...

and therefore, I will say YES to...

Or you can make YES/NO affirmation statements for your week:

This week I say YES to...

This week I say NO to...

Remember to use
YES/NO as your filter
in order to make your
decisions that much
more impactful!

#INSPIRINGINDY

WEEK 37

30 Minutes of Self-Care This Week

It's that time again to focus on loving yourself.

Again, as a reminder, fifteen years of coaching individuals, this is one of the BIGGEST challenges I have listened to from people on all levels—taking time to take care of ourselves.

Hear from Eric Schwefel on how he is 100 percent engaged in transforming people's mindset in using their 30 Minutes of Self-Care to impact their bodies through Schwefel Strength and Performance:

There are so many powerful ways to change a person's body and mindset, yet what has proven to be most effective may not be what you think. When you have the time, set a 20 to 30-minute timer, take 3 deep breaths, and journal. That's right, journal. Journal about your day. Reflect on how you slept, on what you ate, on how you felt after eating. What was your predominant attitude throughout the day? Did you have energy? Why or Why not? The pages are for your taking...

Journaling gives us a chance to "unplug from the matrix" of society and connect with ourselves in a way that few get to experience. Even if it's 5 minutes and the journal is the "Notes" app on your phone, make time to reflect and go within. The inner world creates the outer world. If you are stressed, write it out, reflect, and move forward."

(Eric Schwefel, Schwefel Strength and Performance)

This week for my "30 Minutes of Self-Care," I will:

Say this out loud with me...

It is OK
To Take Care of Myself.

#INSPIRINGINDY

WEEK 38

This Week Go for Victory!

How many times have you heard someone say, "Good luck"?
Going to that important meeting—good luck!
Big event coming up—good luck!
Working on a crucial deal—good luck!

Seemingly going against the odds—good luck! I cannot stand it.

This became apparent to me once I entered into the real estate business eight years ago. It seems that almost EVERYONE tells you "Good luck." It is everywhere you turn—good luck on that deal, good luck with those clients, good luck with THAT house, etc. It feels empty and hollow to me, and I was determined to make a change within our team.

My business partner Gregg Tepper and I take a lot of pride in the fact that we strive to provide excellent service. We have also gone the extra route of taking classes, reading, and studying our business and craft in order to excel in our market. In other words, we don't just wake up in the morning and hope for luck—we work hard to put ourselves in a position to win. And if that is not enough, we weekly put our faith in God by prayerfully inviting Him to show us a path of wisdom for our clients and provision for our families. Saying "Good luck" in this context seems almost laughable to me.

So I proclaimed, "NO MORE GOOD LUCK. From now on, it is 'GO FOR VICTORY!'"

If one is skilled, has done their homework, and has gained wisdom through experience, isn't VICTORY the only logical outcome to be desired?

Going to that important meeting—**Go for Victory** (you did the hard work to get here)!

Big event coming up—**Go for Victory** (you prepared for this day)!

Working on a crucial deal—**Go for victory** (the wisdom you have gained has you ready for this)!

Seemingly going against the odds—**Go for victory** (you are actively participating in your success, and your experience will give you an awareness for whatever the possibility)!

Luck, as it were, only shows up when one is prepared. The saying "I'd rather be lucky than good" does have some credence to it; however, 99 percent of the time, "luck" usually only appears because of your preparation and dedication.

Therefore, I tell you, Go for Victory!

This week I will "Go for Victory" by:

If I am PREPARED... Isn't VICTORY the only logical outcome to be desired?

#INSPIRINGINDY

WEEK 39

Your 8 x 8 Commercial to Make
You a Leader Above the Rest!

Do you know why you forget things? There is a saying, "Out of sight, out of mind" for a reason. And what about another adage, "The squeaky wheel gets the oil"? Why is that the case? Whether it is leadership roles or in our private lives, projects and relationships can get away from us if we do not have consistent "touch" with them. Having a "system" or a "mechanism" in place that you can go to will take the thinking out of what you need to do and make it a part of your routine. Think of this "system" as a playbook for your personal "commercial" for keeping in touch with people or projects that you need to continually touch over a longer period of time. In this example, it is called an "8 x 8," but I have clients who have made it a 6 x 6 or 12 x 12, etc. Whatever the case, you tailor the numbers to your needs.

The following is an example how it could be used to send your commercial to a lead/customer that you want to become your client:

Week 1	Week 2	Week 3	Week 4	Week 5	Week 6	Week 7	Week 8
Call	Video Email	Text	Call	Email	Text	Call	Postcard

In the example above, the potential client is being "touched" once a week over an eight-week period. Remember, this is your commercial. In other words, it is your way of systematically staying in front of your audience.

The following is an example of using your "8 x 8" commercial with groups/areas/people that you need to stay in touch with. Again, remember, it is all about "staying in touch" so that not only does the squeaky wheel get the oil but the quiet groups/areas get TOUCHED by YOUR LEADERSHIP as well.

Connect with:	Week 1	Week 2	Week 3	Week 4	Week 5	Week 6	Week 7	Week 8
Person A	Face-to-Face	Email	Phone Call	Text	Face-to-Face	Email	Phone Call	Text
Person B	Phone Call	Text	Face-to-Face	Email	Phone Call	Text	Face-to-Face	Email
Group A	Email	Phone Call	Text	Face-to-Face	Email	Phone Call	Text	Face-to-Face
Group B	Text	Face-to-Face	Email	Phone Call	Text	Face-to-Face	Email	Phone Call

And, of course, you can use the "8 x 8" for your projects:

Project	Week 1	Week 2	Week 3	Week 4	Week 5	Week 6
Project A	Outline	Connect with Stake Holders	Line up Vendors, Location, etc., Send out "Commercial"	Follow-up with Stake Holders, Send out "Commercial"	Connect with Vendors, tie up loose ends	Roll Out

Remember, the "8 x 8" is a systematic plan to "touch" people and/or projects on a weekly basis to take the thinking out of "What do I do next or where am I in the plan?"

People/Groups/Projects that I could create an "8 x 8" for are:

Connect with:	Week 1	Week 2	Week 3	Week 4	Week 5	Week 6	Week 7	Week 8

Pro Tip: Print out your "8 x 8" and put it on your wall to ensure you have it front and center!

SCOREBOARD

This is your 3rd Quarter Check-up. How are you doing so far with each exercise?

- ☐ Week 27: 30 Minutes of Self-Care: Celebrate a Milestone in Your Life
- ☐ Week 28: Catapult Yourself Out of the Rut
- ☐ Week 29: Invest in Someone's Life
- ☐ Week 30: Action Accelerator Check-In
- ☐ Week 31: Your "Yeah? Watch Me!" Triumph
- ☐ Week 32: Awards Week
- ☐ Week 33: The Big Question for Your Leadership
- ☐ Week 34: Create Magic
- ☐ Week 35: Play Like a Champion
- ☐ Week 36: Yes/No Exercise Accountability Partner
- ☐ Week 37: 30 Minutes of Self-Care
- ☐ Week 38: Go for Victory
- ☐ Week 39: Your 8 x 8 Commercial

WEEK 40

The Week of Building a "Fireproof" Mental Foundation

MENTAL CHALLENGES.
Stress.
Bickering back and forth.
Reacting to "the fires of adversity."

Constant "white noise" yelling in the background.
No one seemingly listening.
Looking for the path of victory through an endless maze of obstacles.

We need to have a way to STAY GROUNDED through the chaos!
A consistent question that I have asked of leadership clients over the years is simple and direct WHO DO YOU WANT TO BE THROUGH YOUR CONFLICTS?

Your answer, in turn, needs to be just as simple and direct in order for you to achieve the impact you are seeking.

An example of this came to fruition from a leadership client when, over the course of a couple of months, we developed their "MENTAL PILLARS OF OPERATION."

In their words, they determined that they wanted to stay grounded to certain ideals that would keep them on their path to success and focused through the stirring chaos.

Their "MENTAL PILLARS OF OPERATION" were "I WILL BE TRUTHFUL, STRONG, CONTENT, AND CONSISTENT."

"I WANT TO BE **TRUTHFUL**" meant they did not have to backtrack down the road or worry about what they said in the past because they spoke the truth in the moment.

"I WANT TO BE **STRONG**" was a reminder they did not want to back down for something that required advocacy rather than cowering back waiting for permission from the opposition.

"I WANT TO BE **CONTENT**" was a cue to stay the course even in the face of adversity because the bottom line spoke to the truth of the matter.

"I WANT TO BE **CONSISTENT**" while others faltered or were not interested. This was a prompt not to give up because the path of least resistance didn't lend a solution—no one will lead the charge more than you, so do not wait for someone else to show up to lead. If you are waiting for a "leader," then that could be a good indication that YOU ARE THE LEADER THAT IS NEEDED **for this moment**.

This week, what are the MENTAL PILLARS OF OPERATION that you want to lead from?

Mental Pillars...

Need to be simple and easy to recall in the heat of the moment for your

Success!

#INSPIRINGINDY

WEEK 41

This Week Put Yourself in the Hall of Fame

Did you know that in professional baseball, if you hit a batting average of .300 and above over a ten-year career, it is highly probable that you would end up in the Hall of Fame? That means you would have to get a hit three times for every ten attempts. This equates to FAILING seven out of ten times! This also displays how difficult it is to hit a baseball that is traveling over ninety-five miles-per-hour in your direction. Win three times out of ten and your name gets enshrined with the greats-of-all-time.

Aren't we up against this in life?

Swinging and missing. Taking the shot, and it bounces out of the rim. Failing.

In sports, it's easy to see this as "part of the game," but in life it can be much harder to manage. I mean, how does one effectively "practice their shot" in life? How does one mentally "stay in the game" when there is no clock or boundaries to seemingly keep us in check?

Use the Hall of Fame Mentality

A professional baseball season has a hundred and sixty-two games. Professional basketball has eighty-two games, and The NFL has sixteen games—all participants prepare in the offseason. How long is your season? For some, if not most, the answer is EVERY DAY. You are in season as a professional, a spouse, a parent, and as a friend. If you show up at all, sometimes you are going to fail or not succeed—be a HALL OF FAMER!

HALL OF FAMERS get back in the batter's box. They don't stop shooting. Michael Jordan, the greatest basketball player of all time, famously said, "You miss 100 percent of the shots you don't take!" In life we must keep playing the game. Failure is going to come, and it is undeniably gut-wrenching when it does. I absolutely, 100 percent, despise losing! It is so dejecting to put your heart and soul into your effort only to see minimal results. However, we must invoke the HALL OF FAME attitude of not giving up.

Didn't get the outcome you were hoping for? Try again!

Didn't have the success you were striving for today? I will tomorrow!

But they told me, "No." We're just getting started. Find out where the "Yes" is.

They threw me a "curve-ball." Use this as experience and go learn how to hit the "curve-ball." Hall of Famers do not stop working on making themselves better.

REMEMBER, ALL YOU NEED TO DO IS GET TO "YES" THREE TIMES OUT OF TEN, AND YOU WILL BE A HALL OF FAMER!

This week I will use my "Hall of Fame Mentality" and get over failure by:

If you have not
received your
7 "NOs"
You are not
trying.

#INSPIRINGINDY

WEEK 42

Alert! This Is Your Final Reminder!

This week, check in with your Action Accelerator Plan.

Yes, that was Week 13, Week 21, and now Week 42.

If you have not checked in with your plan, now is the time to do so.

As a reminder, you chose **4 AREAS OF YOUR LIFE** to focus on and then wrote out the three different columns to complete your Action Accelerator Plan.

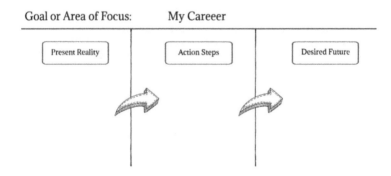

What about your **Week 8 Kick-Starter for Life list**? Have you checked in on those ideas and goals?

Now is the time. Don't beat yourself up if you haven't been able to get started on some of them. Yes, sometimes life does get in the way. However, do not make that an excuse. You know where you have been lazy. You know exactly what you need to do in order to achieve some progress.

LET'S BE HONEST.

If you have not started on some of those ideas or have forgotten them altogether, then maybe it is time to take them off of the list. Or preserve them in safe keeping for later.

Today I want you to simplify your list.

Make it very, very, very simple.

WHAT IS ONE ACTION STEP YOU ARE WILLING TO TAKE FOR YOUR SUCCESS?

Get Started.

#INSPIRINGINDY

WEEK 43

This Week Don't Say "I Wish"

I remember revisiting Wisconsin when I was living in New York City in my late twenties. I was at some gathering and ended up having a conversation with a past high school classmate who was lamenting about choices that they had already made in their young life. The conversation came to a climax when they wistfully retorted, "Don't you wish that you…I don't know…just packed your bags up when you were younger and moved away to a place like New York City?"

I struggled for a moment to sympathize as I nodded my head yes, then the words just fell out of my mouth, "Actually…I did do that."

The conversation did not go very far after that. I felt sorry for them, and I did not want to braggingly do a victory dance all over their unhappiness. They sheepishly responded with an almost empty stare, "Oh…yeah…I guess you did, didn't you?"

They had forgotten that I was living in New York.

Each of us were on the opposite sides of "I wish." They were on the "longing and wondering" side of "I wish," and I was on the "I did it" side of "I wish."

Which side do you want to be on?

There was also the day when I received two life-altering pieces of news in the same hour. The first was a phone call informing me that I was scheduled to have my cancer surgery. The second was from my mom. After I told her my cancer update, she said she was actually getting ready to call me because she had received word that my biological dad was found in a ditch outside of Dallas. He had both a stroke and a heart attack and was on life support. My initial reaction was that I did not want to care. I was more concerned about my surgery.

To process the information, I called my friend Marty to tell him the news. Marty and I had a coaching history together, except this time he was doing the listening. Being who I am, he knew I was open to dialogue—or at least he was testing me out when he profoundly said words to me as if God were speaking directly to me himself, "You know, you got the call that your dad was about to die, not that he died. So you still have a choice."

He nailed it. Game, set, match. The only thing was, I did not want to hear any of it. The little boy in me did not want to care. And I told him that "Marty, I really don't want to hear that today."

We both paused.

What's interesting is that, as I look back, I can see that a healing voice came inside of me during that pause, a voice that wanted to take care of the little boy. I quietly agreed back to Marty, "But you're right. I still do have a choice."

I ended up driving eight hours that day to the hospital in Dallas where my dad was. With each passing hour of the drive, I became a little more nervous. I had no idea what I was going to do or say. This was only the third time in my life seeing the man. The first being when I was fifteen, when he made a surprise stop to my grandparents' ranch in Salmon, Idaho while I was visiting for the first time. He showed up at two-forty-five in the morning, and we met in the middle of the hallway leading to the bedrooms, "Come here, son, give your dad a hug." I obliged.

The second occasion was a more planned trip two years later, as I went back out to Idaho to see my grandparents and spent four days with him and his girlfriend. The trip was highlighted by a three-day camping excursion sleeping in a teepee by a nearby mountain lake.

After this trip, I found out that I was child number six or seven on his long list of children. It was then that I realized that I was really never going to ever have a father in my life. This was just a flash-in-the-pan reunion of sorts. We did not speak again until the day I drove to the hospital. Fourteen years had passed—I was thirty-one years old.

When I arrived at the hospital, visiting hours were almost up, and I wanted to chicken out. But I finally made myself get in the elevator and go up to his floor. Upon the elevator doors opening, I checked with a nurse to see what room he was in, and she led the way to his door as I literally shook with every step.

When I entered the room, I found him hooked up to all kinds of tubes. He wasn't able to speak. I slowly walked around to the right side of his bed away from all of the monitors. It was a perfect moment. It was just the two of us. No bullshit small talk to get in the way. No one else in the room to try to make the mood feel differently than it should. I was finally able to confront the ghost in my life face-to-face. And I did it with grace. I decided it was time to make peace with him and tell him that I forgave him. Most importantly,

I reminded him to ask Jesus for forgiveness of his sins. It was short and sweet. I gave his hand a little squeeze and said goodbye. He died the next week.

I cannot tell you how freeing it is to live and tell that story. I am free and clear of burden, anger, and resentment because I went and made peace with my dad. Yes, I will always have the missing part to my story of not having a father in my life. However, this is not a story about how I wish I would have got past my hurt feelings. This is not a story about how I wish I would have gone to that hospital room and saw my dad one last time. This is not a story about wondering aloud what could have been.

No.

This is a story from the **"I did it" side of "I wish."**

And I want that for you.

This week I will get on the "I did it" side of "I wish" by:

WEEK 44

The Week of Love and Appreciation

Remember the last scene from the movie *"Love Actually"*? It ends with The Beach Boys' song "God Only Knows" playing over a montage of friends and loved ones arriving at the airport, seeing each other for the first time all over again. With each first glimpse, there follows a love and joy that excitedly leaps out of each person involved through bright smiles, hugs, kisses, and warm embraces of all kinds. In that instance, if ever so brief, there is no sadness, anger, stress, or misunderstanding—just a wonderful jolt of happiness. Happiness because I get to see you. Happiness because the drought is over, you're back in my life. Happiness because I have been missing you and we are finally together again.

Gosh, what a beautiful moment.

Love.

I have also taken notice of the Italians that I have been watching on Netflix's documentary series, *Chef's Table*. When it comes to people, they seem to have an extraordinary awareness of love and appreciation through their food preparation and service. If you listen to them tell their stories and watch them work, you can see that they savor each and every element. From ingredients to dining ambiance to the most expensive commodity—time spent—their love and appreciation for people is profound. I even came upon Italian winemaker, Antonio Lamona's LA QUERCIA MONTEPULCIANO D ABBRUZO, who states on the back of his label, "I want to make wines that are pleasing to the body, and the spirit." In effect, I hear him saying, "I'm happy you're here, I want to take care of you while you're here. I want you to enjoy your stay!"

Appreciation.

And yet there are so many times of sadness and loneliness. I can remember when I finally was able to get my own apartment after my divorce. I was not financially able to afford living on my own for a couple of years, and when I finally was able to, I did not have much of anything to furnish it with. I was in my first year of real estate and sleeping on a pullout couch for a couple of months until one glorious day when I found a bed in an old vacant house that I happened to be showing to some clients. It was like God had it waiting for me.

Inside a bedroom was a very wide, closed up closet. When I opened up its double doors, I found a beautiful, hardly touched, red, queen-sized pillow-top mattress and matching box spring. I inquired to the owners of the home if they had any use for the bed, and they said that I could have it. I could not believe it. I used to have my own king-sized plush pillow-top bed and was reduced down to a pullout couch bed with metal springs poking me every night, so this was indeed a big event for me.

And then the loneliness set in. I did not have anyone that could help me with my bed that day. After my divorce, I became so isolated that I did not have a lot of connection with many people. And anyone that I could call was not available. I was also up against time, as this was my only opportunity to get the bed from the house. And let me tell you, getting that queen-sized pillow-top mattress into the bed of my truck was no easy feat. Increasingly daunting was getting that mattress up the very long and steep set of stairs to my second-floor apartment. The cancer surgery on my back that removed a good bit of muscle tissue on my left side only added to my challenge. It took me three tries in sweltering ninety-five-degree heat to get the mattress up that staircase. The first two times ended with the mattress getting three-fourths of the way up only for me to lose grip and slide all the way back down to the first floor. On my last try I was at my wit's end, dripping wet with sweat, half in tears, and wondering how in the heck I ended up in this place of life.

With every last ounce of energy that I had, I pushed that beautiful mattress up each single stair and made the final plunge through the threshold of the living room door. This ended up being my first time sleeping on it, as I laid there for over an hour in utter exhaustion, loneliness, and thankfulness.

Love and sadness, happiness and loneliness, such extreme opposites in the same world. I believe the lesson for us is clear—we are not made in this world to be alone. We are also not made in this world to be self-serving. You cannot have your *Love Actually* moment if you are always getting off of the plane with no one there to greet you.

Equally important is being available to others. If all one ever does is look out for their own needs, not only will they ended up isolated, they will also find themselves on the short end of the love spectrum as well.

Now, it could be easy for me to remember the mattress day and say that I am never going back to that ever again and make the focus all about me. This would place me living life in a scarcity mentality—a mentality that would always be one of fighting, striving, and will never be satisfied.

Instead, I will remember that day with fondness, a hint of fear, and an abundance mentality. I was given a wonderful new bed and opportunity from God to know that I want to help others in their sadness and celebrate in their joys, to appreciate life's little details and…

Love those around me like I just got off of the plane to see them!

@INSPIRINGINDY

This week how do you want to start displaying your LOVE and APPRECIATION?

WEEK 45

The Week of Not Saying Stupid Things to Other People

In other words, think before you speak.

Over the years, I have been told or have heard many off-putting things; some were jarring, while others left little impact. And then there are the negative words that have stuck with me, even some from my own mouth.

To be clear, this is not about silencing people's speech. In today's political arena, speech has become a balance beam with all types of rhetoric jockeying for position. No, I am 100 percent behind freedom of speech. I am also 100 percent behind using wisdom and having discernment in the words that you use in the same turn. That is what this week is all about.

When I was in high school, I worked very hard to make the basketball team. The summer before tryouts, I was told the only guys that would make the team were those who could dribble with both hands. This meant I had to make my left hand as dominant as my right hand. And that is what I did. All summer I did nothing but practice using my left hand at dribbling and shooting. Over a hundred guys tried out for the eighteen-man team, and I was one of them.

At one point during the season, the coach even asked me if I was left-handed. I told him no and that I worked all summer to make sure both of my hands were dominant so that I could make the team. And then he said one of those things that stuck with me: "You know, I have to tell you. You're one of those players that I really don't want to play, but I have to because you work your butt off all the time. Keep up the great work."

What is a fourteen-year-old supposed to say to that? I remember just looking back blankly and saying, "Okay."

The summer going into my sophomore year of high school, I participated in my first away from home football camp. I was not being scouted by college programs by any means, but as far as high school football was concerned, I held my own. There were a couple hundred guys participating in the week-long camp, and each day we were all divided up into groups based on our particular positions. I was in one of three running back groups.

At the end of each day, everyone would gather in an auditorium to have one final meeting which usually consisted of a video or a speaker talking to us about some sort of motivational topic. By the third day, an added wrinkle was presented to us at the end of the day meeting. We were told that coaches would be selecting their all-star player from each group and that we as players had one more day to prove ourselves. Based on my performance and the feedback that I was receiving from the coaches, I had it in the back of my mind that I had a shot at getting the award. There was one other player in my group that seemed to be a stand-out as well. So the competition for the all-star award seemed like it was going to be between the two of us.

The next day we were all in fierce battle mode showing off our skills, and I left no moment for hustle unused. I wanted to be that all-star. Then something curious happened. My competitor did not show up for the afternoon session and completely left the camp, never to be seen again. That evening the running back groups were up for their all-star selections. When it came time for my group to announce its all-star, I braced myself for the final conclusion. And then it happened—my name was announced. I could not believe my ears; I had won the coveted all-star t-shirt. I was beaming with pride.

With the night's festivities over, I headed back to the dorms to go back to my room. When I stepped into the elevator of the dorm, one of my group's assistant coaches was already standing inside. I pressed my floor button and stood there patiently with my all-star t-shirt in my hand as the doors closed. And then the assistant coach said one of those things that stuck with me: "Hey, congratulations again on winning. We were going to give it to that other kid, but he ended up quitting. So we gave it to you."

I almost handed the shirt back to him. I ended up throwing the shirt away when I got back home.

Basketball and football aside, baseball was my chosen sport. I was pretty decent at it having played competitively at various levels since I was eight years old. I had an above-average arm and consistently drove the ball all over the field with a bat. And because I had a good arm and was a leader, I played a lot of catcher because I could throw guys out trying to steal bases. A pitcher on one of my teams even praised my arm strength and thanked me for keeping runners at bay, as he jokingly noted that I threw the ball back harder to him than he actually pitched it.

But not everyone on my team appreciated my baseball abilities. There was one random game where I just had an off day. I was so off that I ended up striking out four times in a row. It was an unusual day for me, and I was quite disappointed. To my astonishment, someone from my team took note of my performance that day and came up to me and said another one of those things that have stuck with me: "Hey, I love it when you have bad days because then I have good days."

Evidently, he managed a couple of hits that day. I don't remember offering much of a comeback for his prideful moment.

My time enduring cancer surgery and treatments also brought out some head scratching moments. After the removal of the tumor in my back, I had to undergo thirty-seven radiation treatments. Treatment consisted of being strapped down to a table with a form-fitted mask put over my face and buttoned down all the way over my shoulders on both sides of my body. Then for the next thirty to forty minutes, I would hear the on-and-off-again crackling of the laser burning through my skin on my back. After a couple of weeks, I couldn't allow for anything to touch the treated area of skin because of the severe burning. I also need to walk with a cane, had difficulty talking, and endured a constant metallic taste in my mouth.

I did have many cards of support and a couple of wonderful people from my business networking group volunteered to drive me to my radiation appointments. And yet, there were people that said things that still have stuck with me to this day. I was consistently targeted by people selling various pills, drinks, and potions to "heal" me, but I was most taken back by the random woman who asked me, "What did you do to manifest cancer in your body?"

I told her I would have to think about that and resumed my quiet position with eyes closed in my waiting room chair of the doctor's office.

During this same period, it was also noted by someone I knew very well that my yard was not being kept up and that "You should really maintain your yard better."

I proceeded the next day to buy a riding lawn mower with the insurance money I received from an Aflac Cancer Insurance policy I had. On the first use, I was so out of it that I did not see the Yellow Pages phonebook that was left at the end of the driveway and ran right over it. Ever see a thick phone book ran over by a riding lawn mower before? It shreds it quite nicely. Pieces of phonebook were everywhere as you can imagine. A neighbor from two doors down must have seen me struggling on my hands and knees because they graciously came over and started to help me pick up the pieces.

Of all of these stories, the one that sticks out the most is the one from my own mouth.

On one particular practice day during my high school senior year of football, I was grouped with all of the defensive linebackers for a tackling drill. The year before, I had been awarded the second team all-conference award for linebackers, so again, I wasn't some big college recruit, but I held my own on the football field. Being a senior and an award winner, one would think that I would have some leadership capabilities and would display them consistently. For the most part I did, however, on this day, I was the one who said those words that have stuck with me till this day. There was another player, a younger player named Nick, who was struggling to do the drill.

Finally, Nick yells out to our Coach, "Coach, what did I do wrong?"

I snidely blurted out in front of the whole group, "You went out for football."

All of the guys laughed.

I felt terrible immediately.

Here was a kid trying his heart out, who at least had the courage to put the pads and helmet on unlike so many other guys I knew, and I made fun of him. I was supposed to be his teammate. I was supposed to be a leader, and I completely blew it for some two-second laugh at his expense. I did go up to him afterwards and apologize, but I still felt awful. I am reminded of that day quite often.

The lesson here I hope is straight forward. Your words have bearing to them. Just because you are thinking something doesn't mean that it needs to be said. Understand your audience and think about the impact your words will have on them in the situation. Remember the "first-person voice" from Week 11? Are you operating from a selfish place or are you building up others with your words? I believe these are important questions to consider if you want to be a leader of people.

This week I will use wisdom in the words and thoughts that come out of my mouth by:

Think Before You Speak

#INSPIRINGINDY

WEEK 46

The Impact Pictures Challenge

Take a look at the pictures on your phone. My guess is that if you are like most people that I see on social media, most of them are you and some other people grouped together in front of some random location. The same pictures over and over of faces smiling back at the camera. Unless you had a caption under the picture, you would not be able to differentiate one picture from the next if you grouped all of the pictures together. Or maybe the pictures are a bunch of pictures of food you made or were eating. Or similarly drinks you were enjoying. If you are honest, most of the pictures are self-serving.

In my world, I have much of the same. I do, however, work hard to have my family members enjoy experiences that I try to capture as a memory on my camera. It drives me crazy to have us just standing like we are a bunch of cutouts—oh, look here, we all are standing in front of *ABC* location, and here we are sitting at *XYZ* location.

And then it struck me about the pictures I was seeing and taking about fishing. All kinds of pictures of all of the fish we caught.

And the animals we hunted. And the drinks we were drinking. And the great places we were visiting. It made me stop one day and say, "Is this what we are meant to do? Are we meant to show off our self-serving ways all of the time?"

I am determined to do better.

And I have to admit, this is a work in progress for me. But I don't want to keep a blind eye to it anymore. This is why I am posing this challenge to both you and to me. This challenge is one that makes you think about how you can create experiences and also offer them to others.

It is the "10 Pictures I Want to Have in the Future That Make a Difference" Challenge.

Of one my pictures that I have planned is one of me feeding people. Instead of showing off my catch and basically saying, "Wow, look at me. I can catch a bunch of fish," I want to show off sharing and enjoying my catch with others. It is also why I always try to invite others with me who don't have the means to go fishing. It is my way of providing experience for other people.

I've taken some great pictures of people on my boat. And here's a little secret—some of them are just mental ones that I have taken. Some of the best are the expressions of people that I have let drive my boat for a few minutes. I get them behind the wheel and gently guide them as they push down the throttle through an open channel. You can see the freedom in their expressions and exhilaration in their voices. What beautiful encounters, and I want more of them for you and for me.

What are the 10 Impactful Pictures that you want to create in the future?

And if you think of it, tag me #inspiringindy or @inspiring-indythelightbulbcoach ;)

1.

2.

3.

4.

5.

6.

7.

8.

9.

10.

WEEK 47

This Week Make Your Process One-Button Simple

I recently read the Steve Jobs biography by Walter Isaacson. I have several takeaways that I have been sharing in my leadership coaching sessions. They range from behavioral dos and don'ts to the creative process to melting down systems and organizational process.

One of Jobs's distinct abilities was to simplify his products in a way that intuitively met his audience and users. If the original gadget was using four screws, he would press the engineers to figure out how to use one screw. The famous iPhone melted all processes down to One-Button—simple, elegant, and easy to use.

Jobs was also very tactile. He demanded that he be able to touch any and all prototypes of future products so that he could get a real sense of the functionality possibilities. Ironically, it seems that he needed to work outside of technology in order to offer technology to the world, as he was infamous for never accepting a PowerPoint presentation but rather dictated that ideas needed to be hashed out in front of the group on a whiteboard.

For my leadership coaching clients, I have been pressing these two ideas together for success in time management and thinking about organizational process. Yes, there are all kinds of apps and programs for time management, but they seem to miss the point of being "one-button simple" and "tactile front and center." If you are a busy executive, manager, or leader on any kind, the last action item you want to add to your day is filling out yet another form to help you with your schedule.

"Tactile front and center" means that you must be able to touch and see it in front of you. It must be easily accessible to use not only to touch it but also an effortless reminder in front of you. In order for this to happen, I suggest my clients get some sort of whiteboard to use as their "playbook." In our real estate office, our team has gone the extra step to actually make one entire wall a dry-erase board with special dry erase paint. This ensures that whenever we look up, we can see our current properties in play and the action steps that are needed or completed in the sales process. A quick glance at the board instantly gets me (and/or others on the team) grounded in our real estate matrix and allows me to think about next steps or check items off of the list and move on to the next client.

A common challenge that is brought up to me in leadership coaching sessions is one of how to get in front of "constantly just putting out fires." This leads to a question of whether or not the leader has a "map" of their workplace environment. Can they "see" the landscape, or is it just a matter of if they remember all of the areas of their leadership? Usually, if it is the latter, the leader is operating in a reactionary mode and off of memory. This creates fertile ground to become a leader that is "always putting out fires" in the workplace. And as I hear often, by this point the "fires" are usually in crisis mode.

Here's my appeal to you: get a whiteboard to create your "playbook" or "map"!

Put it on a wall that you will be able to look up at daily. This is where you write out your playbook action steps. The whiteboard needs to be front and center for easy access. Make the playbook simple. If you need ideas, start with headings such as "High Priority Items," "Medium Priority Items," "Low Priority Items." Or you can have various departments or groups as headings to create your map of influence that you manage. Use color-coordinated sticky notes that can be moved around however you choose to add action items under each heading. Remember, it is your "playbook," so tailor the "playbook" to your needs AND keep it ONE-BUTTON SIMPLE!

What is one area of your life where you can work on being "One Button Simple"?

#INSPIRINGINDY

WEEK 48

The Week of Preparing to be Someone's Superhero

Let's face it, life is hard.

Maybe that is an understatement. It can be downright daunting with many opportunities to say, "I want to give up!" And some do.

I am here to tell you: do not give up. Do not give up because today's challenge is preparing you for something down the road, and that "something" may be to get you ready to be someone's SUPERHERO.

My last day of radiation treatment was a marathon day of not only being buttoned down to the treatment table by the form-fitting mesh mask but also laying inside a tunnel UNDER the mask for over an hour. Weeks earlier, at the beginning of the treatments, when I had to go in the tunnel for the first time, I was asked if I was claustrophobic. Well, I AM NOW!

Going under that mask thirty-seven times for thirty minutes to sometimes over an hour was no easy task. I would often be half in tears trying to endure through the shear mental torture of being buttoned down for so long without any ability to move. One time I was even forgotten in the tunnel and was forced to start screaming for someone to come get me. That was a fun day, let me tell you.

Most sessions I would start out praying the Lord's Prayer over and over in my mind and then I would transition to counting to three hundred because that is how much my Aflac Insurance Policy paid for each torturous treatment session. And then I would wait and wait and wait some more until the crackling of the laser would stop. Once the laser stopped, I would wait for that glorious sound of the door to the radiation room to be kicked open by the technician, which meant they were coming to unbutton me.

The day they forgot me in the tunnel, the crackling laser stopped, and the music in my headset stopped, but there was no voice to tell me that we were finished. And then there was no door being kicked open. And then there was fifteen MORE minutes of complete silence—that is when I truly became anxious. After thirty minutes, absolute panic set in, and I started screaming over and over again for someone to help me. Thankfully, someone was still in the clinic and ran in to get me out of my agony.

Needless to say, wearing that mask was very traumatic for me. I also knew that at the end of my treatments I was going to be asked if I wanted to keep the mask. Now I know what you are probably thinking, "Why on earth would someone want to keep that awful mask?" The only answer I can give is that I had a voice inside tell me that I may need it some day and that I should hold onto it for a little while. Little did I know how soon that moment was going to be.

On that last day of treatment, I was indeed asked if I wanted to keep the mask. I told the technician that I wanted to take it home with me. Upon completion of the treatment, I slowly walked down the hall of the clinic with my cane in one hand and the white mesh mask in the other. When I finally made it to the waiting room, a man jumped up and made a beeline to me. "Excuse me, do you have to wear that mask?" he asked very curiously.

The radiation treatments not only zapped the infected spinal area of my body, they also fried my skin and affected my vocal cords. So with my very raspy voice, I explained that yes, I did have to wear the mask. To my amazement, this man was so thankful that I was there to talk to him about wearing the mask. He asked me several questions about my experience and what I had to go through. It turned out that this was his first day of treatments, and he was filled with all kinds of fear and anxiety—especially about wearing the mask. He told me that I was the only person that he was able to start talking to about what he was feeling and that he was totally relieved to be able to talk with me. He shared with me that he had a brain tumor of some kind and that he was told that by the end of his treatments it was highly probable that he would lose sight in both of his eyes. He also lamented that the worst part about it for him was that he would not be able to see his daughter walk down the aisle when she got married.

Listening to that man speak, and later hugging me for being there for him, certainly put carrying that mask in a completely different perspective for me. Here I was worried about how the mask was going to affect *me*, I had absolutely no idea how I would actually be someone's superhero because of it.

By now, if you have not caught onto one of the themes of this book, you haven't been paying attention. We are not here in this world to be self-serving celebrities in our own narcissistic world. And that includes our times of troubles and tribulations. I believe it is these very times that prepare us for when it comes time for *us* to be the life preserver in other people's lives. Our troubling experience may be the exact prerequisite training in order for us to be equipped to help someone else who may need a strong helping hand in the future.

I have also seen it time and time again in leadership coaching clients of mine, who, going through challenging times at work, would handle an even larger challenge down the road seemingly with ease because they were prepared a year or two earlier. I have been known to be a sort of "prophet" with some of my leadership clients as I have foreseen their current hardship in light of what I thought their futures to be by telling them, "You are being prepared for something bigger down the road!"

I have yet to be let down after saying that. Most clients are promoted to bigger titles with more complexity or have even transitioned into larger roles outside of their current career altogether.

So I tell you now: **do not give up**. You are being prepared for something bigger down the road. One day you just might end up being someone's superhero just at the right time.

This week, how can you look at your hardships and challenges differently?

What might you be being prepared for?

Today's Challenge... is preparing you for something down the road.

#INSPIRINGINDY

WEEK 49

Heavy Lifting: Know Your Influences

Do you want to become not only a LEADER but a GREAT LEADER?
Become self-aware.

Start to have an awareness of how you affect people—how you affect the room you enter, how you come across to others when you speak, listen, ask questions, act in times of stress or even how you participate in other's success. Pay attention to how you interact with the world around you.

One way I suggest to start paying attention to yourself is by listing out and taking note of your personal influences, both positive and negative. This will help you take a very deep dive inventory as to how you have been shaped up to this point in your life. You may find some "Ah-ha" moments as you reflect on some of the people that have come in and out of your life. You may also find yourself saying, "You know, that's maybe why I do..." or "Maybe that's why I don't..."

How many times have you heard a story by someone that is a variation of "My parents or grandparents used to do that so now I do that"? A certain cycle seems to get repeated and sometimes not for the better. "So-and-so was an alcoholic and beat or neglected us as kids, and now I can see myself slipping into that same pattern" and other similar stories may be ones that you have heard. The cycles can easily repeat themselves unless some sort of intervention mechanism is in place. In my life, I have used the "Know Your Influence" exercise to understand certain negative cycles or influences so that I do not perpetuate them with my circle of influence or loved ones.

An example of this is found in some of the men in my life. My grandfather on my mother's side was born to a very young mother and for the most part, was emotionally neglected for the early part of his life. This disinterest followed him all the way into his enlisting in the United States Navy. Upon my grandfather going away to WWII, it was as if she wrote him off immediately, as she sold all of his belongings and gave away his bedroom to a new baby sibling. When his time of service was up, and he returned home, he was met with shock as he found all of his belongings gone and was told he was thought to be "dead in the war." Needless to say, he didn't stay very long.

As a member of the "greatest generation," he was a hard and dedicated worker who provided for his inner circle. At age fifty-three, he retired on his pension and got busy in his new hobby of wood carving, almost as a second career. He went onto live until age ninety. The only real thing I remember of him was that he was fun at major family gatherings and that when I was twenty-six year old, living in New York City, he called me and apologized for ignoring me when I was growing up. I was his only grandson.

I think because of the way he grew up, he learned to be very self-sufficient but also learned not to go too far outside of his circle because of the hurt that he endured from his closest family or lack thereof. He golfed, bowled, wood-carved, and read—all individual activities that one was rarely invited into. The insight I gained from this influence was to not perpetuate that hurt into my life. I did not want to continue the "individual activity syndrome" into my life. Walk into my house on any given weekend, when all seven of my immediate family members are together, and you will find I am very involved but not too involved as to not give everyone their needed space. Whether it is playing games, cooking, gardening, and even cleaning, I seek to have a real sense of team, moments of learning together, and playfulness.

Another man in my library of influences was my mom's third husband. He was my stepdad for eleven years. He was a very cold man, and I seldom wanted to be in the same room with him. I equated being around this man at how I would imagine Storm Troopers from the movie Star Wars felt when Darth Vader walked into their presence—with fear and dread.

Again, here was another man who was mistreated as a boy, who found little love and nourishment from his family, and it was passed on through his parenting. He would often have me and my two step-brothers "help" in the yard and the gardening. "Helping" usually consisted of watching him do all of the digging, planting, and watering and then for us boys to be told to "pick up the tools." There was also the time when we were asked to "help" make the picnic table. "Helping" consisted of watching him as he measured and cut the wood, nailed the wood in place, and finally painted the table only for us to be finally told to "pick up the tools." When I was old enough to start wearing ties, he even had a hard time wanting to teach me how to tie a tie because he did not want to "ruin his ties."

So what was the influence? I did not want to perpetuate the negative behavior. I was and am determined to be a parent and a teacher who is self-aware to involve participants in the process. Ironically, this is one thing I learned from him because he taught me how to do one thing well—he taught me how to ride a bike. In teaching me to ride a bike, unlike the other chores or activities which he could just do himself, he had to involve me in the process because he had to get *me* on the bike. He then proceeded to hold me and guide me on the bike. And when I eventually fell, he was there to put me back on the bike and start the process all over again until I finally was able to successfully ride by myself.

Now I get others to "ride the bike" in life. Helping co-create a mission church in New York City and start an English-as-a-second-language program along with my leadership coaching for the past fifteen years is a direct result of learning from this influence. Also, up until about four years ago, I couldn't care less about yard work or gardening, but now I have my wonderful wife to enjoy it with, and I get my children involved in every step.

My third son Micah, who is twelve, even told me that he takes pride in his hard work of helping trim trees and mowing the lawn with me. I don't really have an aptitude for woodworking or building, but I have recognized it in my older son Indy, so I get him heavily involved in fixing "stuff." It was an exceptionally proud day for me when I empowered both him and my second son Noah to completely set up the new mailbox, which consisted of using a skill saw, drill, hammer, and nails! And because I knew what it felt like not to be able to tie my own tie, when I was working with the troubled youth at the Youth Service Bureau, I added a section to my social skills class of "dressing for success," which not only taught each student how to tie a tie but also gave them one as a gift.

So what is the lesson? I could have easily continued the negative cycles, but instead, I did the work to become self-aware. I looked into my influences and learned from them, even the ones that left me with pain or disappointment. And I turned those influencing lessons into powerful generators to make the world I touch a better place. This process also ensures that I am able to snuff out any so-called "blind spots" or at the very least, be open to exploring them rather than hide from them due to my insecurity. If ever there was a culprit to point at for perpetuating the negative cycle, I believe insecurity would be very close to the top of the list. So let me encourage you, find the courage inside of you to look at your "influencers" and see what self-awareness can be uncovered. The world that you touch just might become a little bit better as a result.

Are you keeping alive
the
Good Behaviors
or the
Bad Behaviors
that have influenced
your life?

#INSPIRINGINDY

My list of people who have influenced me—either positively or negatively—in my life up to this point are:

Consider the following:
What can I learn from their influence?

Are there any behaviors that I am continuing—good or bad?

Is there an insecurity that I am hiding behind that is holding me back from moving forward in my life?

How can I use my influencing to make my world a better place?

WEEK 50

Heavy Lifting: Prepare for the Next Best Chapter of Your Life

I have heard it said to understand where you are going, you need to understand where you have been. Or from Tom Hanks's character,

Forest Gump, "There's an awful lot you can tell about a person by their shoes. Where they're going, where they've been."

This week I want you to write out a bullet-point list of where "your shoes have been" by highlighting both the good and the bad, the highs and the lows of your life journey thus far. This is yet another way of mentally checking in with yourself. It is also a way of creating a baseline for your future growth.

THE BULLET-POINT HIGHS AND LOWS OF MY LIFE:
(Start writing, don't over think this)

When you are complete with your list, consider:

WHERE CAN YOU CELEBRATE?

WHAT ARE YOUR "LIGHTBULB" MOMENTS?

DO YOU NOTICE ANY PATTERNS?

DO YOU SEE ANY POSSIBILITIES FOR YOUR CHANGE?

WHO ARE PEOPLE THAT COULD BENEFIT FROM YOUR REARVIEW MIRROR LIST?

WHERE DO YOU WANT YOUR STORY TO GO FROM HERE?

WEEK 51

Heavy Lifting: Meet Your Future Self

Have you met Fisherman Fred? He truly is an intriguing man. If you go looking for him, you will find he is at his mountain ranch in Idaho, sitting in a sturdy old wooden rocking chair on the covered back patio, sipping something tasty as he gazes out over his pasture with boldly beautiful mountains keeping him company in the not-so-far-off horizon. His posture is relaxed and sure as he sits in his blue jeans and loose-fitting, half-buttoned-down white shirt. His worn boots give notice that he's up for the task, but he won't presume anything, he'll wait to be invited.

Next to him, he always has an open chair to join in his presence. You see, Fisherman Fred is a man that has a past. And as you catch a glimpse of his dark brown eyes looking right back at you, they share just that—a past of adventures, of hardships, of laughs, of love; a past of knowledge to contribute if you take the time to listen. And just like any good fisherman, he knows "where to go and where not to go, what they're biting on and what not to waste your time on." Fisherman Fred is a man you want to pull up a chair to before you go out into the water. But don't be fooled, his waters are not really just fishing waters, they are the waters of life—and you would do well to pay attention to the wisdom offered. This is Fisherman Fred, and he is my future self.

Find Your Future Self

I discovered Fisherman Fred years ago in my coaching training through the "Meet Your Future-Self" exercise of the fulfillment portion of the class. *The purpose of meeting your "future self" is to tap into the essence of who it is you want to be in this world or how you want to interact with the world around you at your most fulfilling self.* The gift then is to take these qualities, these traits, and put them to work into who you are today. Not to get too caught up in my own self abilities, I also couple "future self" with God's inspired words for my life in the Bible and therefore, truly have a focused and exceptional manner in which to touch the world before me.

Now it is your turn.

Take a moment to visualize and let your mind's eye go into the future—twenty years into the future. As you take this moment, allow yourself to take a deep cleansing breath, in and out, in order to let your thoughts go freely through the exercise…

If you were able to transport yourself twenty years into the future, where would you end up landing? What would the landscape look like? And if you walked this landscape for a moment, and you came upon yourself—a twenty years older version of your self—who would you find? What would they look like? How would they sound? When your future self invites you to have a conversation, what wisdom would they impart to you? And when you asked your future self what message of hope they had for you, what message would that be? And then, once you digested the significance of meeting your future self, you realized they had a different name other than your own, a name that was a touch-stone of their fulfilling essence, what would be the name your future self tells you?

Take in all of the details. This is the gift of your future self to occupy your daily life's gestures in the present moment. And not only to enjoy as a gift, but for you to BE THE GIFT as well.

Take time now to reflect upon your future self. Write those thoughts down below, and remember, don't forget your future self's unique name!

MY FUTURE-SELF
(Start Writing)

**Start Living
Your
"Future-Self"
Today!**

WEEK 52

The Week of Being a Part of Something Larger Than Yourself

One maintenance job that requires a lot of effort on my part is painting. To be frank, I don't enjoy painting walls, trim, ceilings, etc., and I am not altogether that great at it either. My wife on the other hand loves to paint. She enjoys picking out the colors, prepping the area, and then transforming the room into a new existence.

So when she came to me with the idea of painting the front exterior stucco wall of our house and the front door, all I heard was WORK THAT I DID NOT WANT TO DO. This coupled with the fact that I have a very bad back made a very easy case for me to not be involved. If she wanted to do this so badly, I would help pick out the paint and keep her company while she pressed on, and that would be the extent to my help.

She didn't mind at all. It was just something she had in her mind to do with or without me. Once we came home with the paint, she immediately went to work. But then it dawned on me—this was a moment to support my wife and BE A PART OF HER PROCESS. At first all I did was get a chair and sit out with her to keep her company. Eventually, I helped move the ladder, and then, yep you guessed it—I started painting. Obviously, the process moved along a lot faster because I joined in, but the greatest benefit was what it did for my wife—she felt supported—and we bonded over the moment of transforming the front of our home together.

And I almost blew it.

Fortunately, I seized the moment to see an opportunity to be a part of something LARGER THAN ME.

Isn't it ironic the things we want—fulfillment, connection, joy—elude us the more we focus on ourselves? It is my belief that God planted in each and every one of us this feeling of true joyfulness when we take care of or join in with others and their process. There is no other explanation for where the satisfaction comes from by lending a helping hand and seeing the dividends it pays. Only a loving God can foster such an innate desire of His creation to care for itself. If we just randomly showed up on this planet, with no rhyme or reason, no purpose, why on earth would we care or find gratification in helping our fellow neighbor?

And just as I am imploring you to seek out opportunity to be a part of something LARGER THAN YOURSELF, I too am doing the same. I have several reasons for writing this book. I have a deep built-in desire to help people and empower them to new heights so that they can live rich, rewarding lives. I also want people who come into contact with this book to discover the true riches of heaven awaiting them through our Savior, Jesus Christ.

And finally, I want to raise money to help others in their process. One such organization that is much LARGER THAN ME that I will be supporting with some of the proceeds from this book is James Samaritan in Covington, Louisiana. When foster children need help or age out of the system, James Samaritan is there to bridge the gap for these youth to adulthood. They are not just in business to be in business, they truly are making a difference. You can find out about them at www.jamessamaritan.org.

It is my prayer that this book can make a difference not only in your life but also in the lives of the youth it can monetarily support. To that end, **"Get out of your head and into your life!"**

184

Fulfillment
Connection
and
Joy
Await You!

 #INSPIRINGINDY

Scoreboard

This is your 4th Quarter Check-up. How are you doing so far with each exercise?

- ☐ Week 40: Fireproof Mental Foundation
- ☐ Week 41: Become a Hall of Famer
- ☐ Week 42: Final Action-Planner Reminder
- ☐ Week 43: Don't Say I Wish
- ☐ Week 44: Love and Appreciation
- ☐ Week 45: Not Saying Stupid Things
- ☐ Week 46: Impact Pictures
- ☐ Week 47: One-Button Simple
- ☐ Week 48: Preparing to Be Someone's Superhero
- ☐ Week 49: Know Your Influences
- ☐ Week 50: The Next Best Chapter of Your Life
- ☐ Week 51: Meet Your Future-Self
- ☐ Week 52: Be a Part of Something Larger Than Yourself

LAGNIAPPE

What I Really Want You to Know

We have just concluded an extraordinary fifty-two-week journey together of exploration, discovery, and hopefully, fantastic results. **You could very well stop here and be on your way.** I would, however, be remiss in my job as a "trusted guide" if I didn't present to you the actual fuel I use in my daily existence and the true guide behind all of my ideas.

You see, left to my own abilities and capabilities, my depth for wanting to work with people on any level is quite shallow and come to think of it, can be very selfish, only seeking what is a beneficial outcome for my position. Further, when my position is for the most part self-seeking or self-serving, the results are not that fulfilling or gratifying and ultimately all I am left with is "Is this it?"

The conclusion I am met with is that I need a deeper well of resource—a well that not only gives ability to truly connect and advocate unselfishly but also one of real, lasting fulfillment. That unending well of nourishment is none other than Jesus Christ, the Savior of the world.

When confronted with the fact that Jesus loved me first and STILL loves me through my ups and downs, it helps me in times when dealing with people who are frustrating to deal with. Looking in my rearview mirror, I know that my behavior indeed can be frustrating to HIM, and yet HE still forgives me when I repent to HIM. *If I can be forgiven, can't I be gracious to others as well?* When HIS WORD

187

tells me HE is slow to anger, isn't this cause for me to pause as well when emotion strikes? When HIS WORD tells me, HE paid the ultimate price for not only me, but all of humanity, this is the well to reach into when others have caused me pain and I need to find the ability to forgive.

And if THAT is not enough to provoke, there are the words from HIS WORD in the gospel of Matthew chapter 25 that let us in on the reward awaiting us for looking outside of ourselves:

> **Then the King will say to those on his right, "Come, you who are blessed by my Father; take your inheritance, the kingdom prepared for you since the creation of the world. For I was hungry and you gave me something to eat, I was thirsty and you gave me something to drink, I was a stranger and you invited me in, I needed clothes and you clothed me, I was sick and you looked after me, I was in prison and you came to visit me."**
>
> **Then the righteous will answer him, "Lord, when did we see you hungry and feed you, or thirsty and give you something to drink? When did we see you a stranger and invite you in, or needing clothes and clothe you? When did we see you sick or in prison and go to visit you?"**
>
> **The King will reply, "Truly I tell you, whatever you did for one of the least of these brothers and sisters of mine, you did for me."**

When Jesus becomes the object of our affection, love, desire, and purpose, the well to tap into is UNENDING. The results are consistently the same—I never become too empty to help others or to find fulfillment in my life.

Your Secret Weapon for Burnout

Let me reiterate, if all we do is seek satisfaction and motivation from inside of this world, we will eventually be let down, either by people or the compensation—we will burnout. We will burnout at work and at home. However, did you know the Bible already has a "burnout eliminator program" in place?

> **Whatever you do, work at it with all your heart, as working for the Lord, not for human masters, 24 since you know that you will receive an inheritance from the Lord as a reward. It is the Lord Christ you are serving. (Colossians 3:23–24)**

Let Jesus be your motivation! Let Jesus be your well of energy!

He is your secret weapon!

Finally, it would be scary for me to see you excel in all of the fifty-two-week exercises of this world but not be prepared for the world to come which will last for eternity. If you didn't make it to heaven and found out that I was sitting on THAT knowledge, THAT exercise, you would be tremendously hurt and angry with me.

Jesus's words from the gospel of John chapter 12, verse 47 remind us we are all on notice:

> **If anyone hears my words but does not keep them, I do not judge that person. For I did not come to judge the world, but to save the world. There is a judge for the one who rejects me and does not accept my words; the very words I have spoken will condemn them at the last day.**

AND maybe I am being self-serving with my eternal inheritance, however, when the KING speaks, I listen to HIS direction from the gospel of Matthew 10:

> **Therefore everyone who confesses Me before men, I will also confess him before My Father in heaven. But whoever denies Me before men, I will also deny him before My Father in heaven.**

This is my confession.

I am fully vested.

It is my hope and
prayer that you will
be too.

 #INSPIRINGINDY

Believe in Jesus, the Son of God, He Is the Only Way to Eternal Life

Jesus was a real man; the historical evidence is overwhelming and well-documented. Therefore, HE was either a lunatic or truly what HE said HE was THE SON OF GOD WHO CAME TO SAVE THE WORLD.

How many timeless books are written with precision accuracy about a lunatic anyway?

Jesus answered, "I am the way and the truth and the life. No one comes to the Father except through me. If you really know me, you will know my Father as well. From now on, you do know him and have seen him." (John 14:6)

I am the gate; whoever enters through me will be saved. (John 10:9a)

For God so loved the world that he gave his one and only Son, that whoever believes in him shall not perish but have eternal life. For God did not send his Son into the world to condemn the world, but to save the world through him. Whoever believes in him is not condemned, but whoever does not believe stands condemned already because they have not believed in the name of God's one and only Son. (John 3:16)

Let Go and Submit...You Will Find Peace

IF YOU ARE RELYING ON YOURSELF, YOU ARE DOING TOO MUCH
OF THE HEAVY LIFTING. AND YOU ARE PROBABLY DOING IT ALL WRONG
ANYWAY IN YOUR ARROGANCE, NOT TO MENTION MISSING OUT ON THE
BLESSINGS THAT COULD BE YOURS.

Do not be stiff-necked, as your ancestors were; submit to the Lord. Come to his sanctuary, which he has consecrated forever. Serve the Lord your God, so that his fierce anger will turn away from you. If you return to the Lord, then your fellow Israelites and your children will be shown compassion by their captors and will return to this land, for the Lord your God is gracious and compassionate. He will not turn his face from you if you return to him. (2 Chronicles 2:30)

Trust in the Lord with all your heart and lean not on your own understanding; 6 in all your ways submit to him, and he will make your paths straight. (Proverbs 3:5)

The Lord is near. Do not be anxious about anything, but in every situation, by prayer and petition, with thanksgiving, present your requests to God. And the peace of God, which transcends all understanding, will guard your hearts and your minds in Christ Jesus. (Philippians 5:7)

Do not love the world or anything in the world. If anyone loves the world, love for the Father is not in them... The world and its desires pass

away, but whoever does the will of God lives forever. (1 John 2: 15, 17)

Take to Heart
the Parable of
The
10 **Virgins...**

The Doors Will Close...Will You Be Locked Out?

Back when I was a staff minister in New York City at Sure Foundation Lutheran Church, and before I had a car, I had to use the subway as my transportation. There was one evening I was making my way back home on the subway when I arrived to the station and was pleasantly surprised that there was a train already waiting. With the doors open to the cars, I found myself a seat and patiently waited for the doors to close and for the train to shuttle me to my next stop. For some unknown reason, the train remained stationary for another fifteen minutes or so. While I was waiting, I began to read the section of the Bible that I was going to be leading in service the next day. That section was the parable of the ten virgins from the gospel of Matthew 25:1–13.

What was remarkable to me that evening was how the parable came to life on that train platform in front of my very eyes. Literally, as I was reading verse 11, the doors of the train closed, and people came running up to the doors pounding on them as I read, "Later the others also came, 'Lord, Lord,' they said, 'open the doors for us!' But he replied, 'I tell you I don't know you.'"

The train left the station.

Those people were left behind. That is how it will be if you do not heed God's word.

The Parable of the Ten Virgins from the Gospel of Matthew Chapter 25

At that time the kingdom of heaven will be like ten virgins who took their lamps and went out to meet the bridegroom. Five of them were foolish and five were wise. The foolish ones took their lamps but did not take any oil with them. The wise ones, however, took oil in jars along with their lamps. The bridegroom was a long time in coming, and they all became drowsy and fell asleep. At midnight the cry rang out: "Here's the bridegroom! Come out to meet him!"

Then all the virgins woke up and trimmed their lamps. The foolish ones said to the wise, "Give us some of your oil; our lamps are going out." "No," they replied, "there may not be enough for both us and you. Instead, go to those who sell oil and buy some for yourselves." But while they were on their way to buy the oil, the bridegroom arrived. The virgins who were ready went in with him to the wedding banquet. And the door was shut. Later the others also came. "Lord, Lord," they said, "open the door for us!" But he replied, "Truly I tell you, I don't know you."

Therefore keep watch, because you do not know the day or the hour.

Next Steps:

THE BOOK OF ACTS 16:31–32:

"Sirs, what must I do to be saved?"
They replied, "Believe in the Lord
Jesus, and you will be saved—you and your
household."

PRO TIP: FIND A BIBLE-TEACHING CONFESSIONAL CHURCH IN YOUR AREA AND START ATTENDING.

"The Wilderness Moment"

GOD HAS A HISTORY OF TAKING HIS PEOPLE "OUT INTO THE WILDER-
NESS" IN ORDER TO CALL THEM CLOSER TO HIM AND COMPLETE THEIR
TRAINING.
   IS HE DOING THIS TO YOU?

-   Adam was literally formed in the wilderness.
-   Abraham had to be taken to a new land—there he would
    become the father of God's chosen people.
-   Isaac wrestled with GOD out in the dessert.
-   Moses fled Pharaoh's palace and lived into the dessert for
    over forty years before GOD gave him his orders.
-   Ruth had to be taken to a new land in order for her to
    receive her blessing and forever be connected to the ances-
    try of Jesus which perfectly fulfilled the prophecy of the
    Bible.
-   King David spent many a night out in the wilderness as a
    shepherd boy.
-   The prophet Elijah spent many days alone in caves and the
    wilderness before he was summoned to be GOD's messen-
    ger and have his historic showdown with King Ahab.
-   Jonah tried running away from GOD's call to him, so GOD
    singled him out and made him very uncomfortable until
    he obeyed.
-   John the Baptist lived a life in the wilderness and was set
    apart to be the signal of the coming Savior of the world

- Jesus, in preparation for his ministry, was taken out into the wilderness for forty days and forty nights to fast and be tempted by the devil.

Are you going through a period of hardship? Are you going through a time in your life where you feel you are stuck and cannot move forward? Do the actions you take seem to only result in a dead end? Are you feeling isolated and alone?

If you are able to identify with these or similar circumstances you may, in fact, be in a "wilderness moment." A moment where God is taking you out of your situation in order to get your attention. A moment to call you to HIM. If He cannot get your attention, you will never change into the person that He wants you to become. And in order for God to get our attention, that more than likely requires some sort of pain for us to go through, or paraphrasing the remarkable, converted Christian author, C.S. Lewis, who himself was once an atheist:

"God's megaphone to the heart is—pain."

My definitive "wilderness moment" lasted four years. Four years of barely paying my bills, getting by on the bare minimum. Four years of losing out on well-paying, career jobs because I was told I was "over-qualified," "Your *third* personality profile that you took just doesn't match who we are," or my favorite, "We just think you would be bored after a while." I even had an interview question that asked me if "I had conquered my boogieman yet." Four years of going in and out of relationships that never matched up. Four years of spending hour upon hour staring out at trees while swimming through my head seeking for answers. Four years of reading, crying, writing, praying, searching, and finally becoming silent.

The biggest learning for me in my "wilderness moment" was that God had to root out the co-dependency I had in my life. In order for me to move forward in my life, to truly get on my feet and be the vessel that God intended me to be, I had to learn how to deal with emotional pain in my life.

Pain is an interesting obstruction in our lives. No one likes pain; we try to get rid of it as soon as we feel it. This usually results in us hunting to fill or numb our pain with things *other* than God—drugs, alcohol, hobbies, sex, work, adventure seeking, etc. I can remember when my co-ed soccer games would be canceled because of weather, and I would be beside myself. I would get mad at God, yelling, "God, you KNEW how much I was looking forward to the game this week! You couldn't stop the rain for one day?"

I was mad because at the time, this was the way I was numbing my pain. For two to four hours a week, during a three-month season, all that I concentrated on was running around trying to exhaust myself chasing after a stupid soccer ball.

The same pattern appeared in searching for jobs, dating women, and my obsession with tango; I was trying to fill my pain with things and people. It wasn't until I finally realized I needed to invite Jesus into my pain that my life started to change and find peace. I literally prayed the words, "Jesus please come into my pain" over and over and over again. I would also ask Jesus to send me a "team of healing angels" to help heal me every night when I went to sleep. And I started to read the Bible and pray differently. When I read the Bible, it was about GOD filling me up. When I prayed, my focus was about asking GOD to fill in my emptiness. The words of Martin Luther I remembered hearing back in my school days came alive in my life: **"It is God's way to empty us before he can fill us up."**

I needed to be emptied.
It was quite painful.

I also learned to get quite and truly listen. The words of Psalms 46:10 grounded me: **He says, "Be still, and know that I am God."**

Going through a "wilderness moment" is not easy. It is not intended to be. Sometimes repeat visits to the "wilderness" are necessary. It is a time to melt us down. It is a time of initiating our hearts and minds. More than likely, it is a time of pain. Full renovation usually requires letting go of old ways, habits, or people.

And this cannot be overstated enough—if indeed God is rooting something out of you in this "wilderness moment," then it may take some time to truly get rid of it. This is all in an effort to ensure you do not regress back to your old-self once your "wilderness moment" is complete. A full cleansing will bring you to a place of looking at your old self and not wanting to return to that old pattern of life. I have found in my life that God usually hands back the test to me until I pass—and He wants us all to pass the test (the blessings are so much better once you do). Passing the test almost always demands me to fully trust His ways, His timeline, and letting go of anything I place before Him.

If you find yourself in a "wilderness moment," take heart, and know that you may very well be being prepared for a transformation down the road. Remember, more than likely, this is a time of God calling you to HIM.

- **Don't miss the opportunity.**
- **Take a moment to thank God for this time in your life.**
- **Invite Him into your pain.**
- **Make Jesus the object of your desire, love, and affection.**
- **Be ready to let go of old ways.**
- **Peace is waiting for you.**
- **Heart healing: Start reading the Book of Psalms in the Bible.**

What thoughts are provoked in you after reading about the "wilderness moment"?

Your "Wilderness Moment" Prayer

I am a lifelong Lutheran. I have attended both Wisconsin and Missouri Synod churches since I was born. I even played a young Martin Luther in a grade-school play when I was in kindergarten. So it is safe to say he has rubbed off on me a little.

It is because of Martin Luther there was not only a reformation of the church but also, everyday people were able to touch the Holy Scriptures because of his translating the Word into the common language of his day. Dig a little into his story, and you will find he certainly had his "wilderness moment" before he became such a prominent character in history.

Luther's foundational reformation of the Christian church whittled Christianity down to three main pillars of belief, that is, Christians believe *salvation is obtained by grace alone, scripture alone, and faith alone.* These three pillars were the culmination of a life that once struggled with uncertainty of salvation from a youth not fully grounded in Scripture to one that found peace once he thoroughly examined them.

And being the well-rounded theologian that he was, Luther was concerned with understanding our faith, as well as connecting to our "faith-giver" through prayer. Just like his three pillars, he is known for his "Four Stranded Prayer," a prayer outline that is straight forward and to the point, always making the prayer point to the author and perfecter of our faith, Jesus Christ. While I was a staff-minister in New York City, I was reminded by Pastor Steve Gabb who I worked with, about Martin Luther's "Four Stranded Prayer." I always appreciate this prayer as a wonderful "prayer paradigm" especially in times when I know I want to pray but don't know exactly how to form my prayer.

I invite you to pray with these four "strands" in mind as we are reminded by the apostle Paul in his epistle to the Ephesians, chapter 6, verse 18: **"[P]ray in the Spirit on all occasions with all kinds of prayers and requests. With this in mind, be alert and always keep on praying for all the Lord's people."**

ARE YOU BEING
CALLED?

IS IT TIME TO
GET SILENT
&
LISTEN
DIFFERENTLY?

WHETHER IT BE A PORTION OF THE BIBLE THAT YOU ARE REFLECTING ON OR A CIRCUMSTANCE OF YOUR LIFE, USE THESE "FOUR STRANDS" AS YOUR GUIDE TO A FULL AND FOCUSED PRAYER DURING YOUR "WILDERNESS MOMENT."

INSTRUCTION

Lord, what are you wanting to teach me regarding (this situation in my life)? What is the lesson or knowledge you would have me know?

THANKSGIVING

Lord, as I reflect on this season in my life, I need to take time to thank you for…

Lord, as I also ponder this moment in my life, I recognize that I don't always live my life as you would have me to, therefore, I need to confess and repent of (sin)...in my life. Because of Jesus's death and resurrection, please forgive me.

Lord, I am asking you to help me with...but not as I will, your will be done.

My "Wilderness Moment" Prayer

DEAR HEAVENLY FATHER...

IN JESUS'S NAME,
AMEN.

My Prayer for Wisdom

Each and every week I am presented with many scenarios that require acute attention, guidance, and wisdom.

As a leadership coach, I work with other leaders who seek me out to assist in navigating their stressful situations, decision-making, and management landscapes.

As a top-performing real estate agent, I engage in evaluating properties with and for clients. This is done simultaneously while tactfully negotiating not only winning contracts but also personalities and situations of all kinds that may or may not have started off on the "right foot." In the end, these clients need me to be their trusted guide in what probably will be the largest financial decision of their lives.

And finally, I am a husband and father, who seeks to love, lead, guide, and provide for his family—they are my "corner of the world" that I have been entrusted with, and I want to care for them as best as I can.

I do not take any of these platforms lightly nor am I arrogant to think that I am singularly endowed with enough wisdom and knowledge on my own to be a guiding light for each. It would be foolish to rely solely on my experience, skills, and training and think it sufficient for the deep and wide-ranging needs and pressures that come at me each and every day. This, coupled with the fact that I want long-lasting, over-the-top results for each means that I must seek wisdom and knowledge outside of myself, I must ask God, my Creator, for HIS wisdom.

And I do, every day with prayer. I also read at least one Bible passage to start my day off right (it's usually the "passage of the day" from my Bible app). I want to be the best I can be for my family and those I work for and with. In order to do that, I recognize that I need God's words in me, not my own.

The results never cease to amaze me. I am consistently met with "Wow, I never would have thought of that" or "Thank you for that insight, I needed a new way of seeing this." Or in situations that seemingly have no real good ending in sight, there I am with a way to navigate through the stress and get the client moving on with the rest of their life.

For added insight, hear now from someone that I admire, a man that recognizes the importance of true wisdom—God-inspired wisdom—Captain Michael Bopp, president of The Crescent River Port Pilot's Association. Captain Bopp's leadership is in charge of hundreds, if not thousands, of lives that interact on the Mississippi River on a daily basis.

We live in a world that influences us in many ways, and yet the word of God has stood the test of time, and is the true instruction on how to live. The world's view on things has never remained the same and has changed drastically along the way, which is why we should never totally lean on our own wisdom in walking through life. God has blessed us with the attribute of knowledge and wisdom to live our lives, yet know, these attributes are very finite. God does put challenges and difficult decisions in the paths of our lives so we can grow in Christ. Being a pilot, on ships that are sometimes longer than three football fields, can be very challenging. Experience becomes so valuable. Sometimes these decisions have to be made under very extreme conditions and, if incorrectly measured, they can have grave outcomes. We have a huge responsibility to protect the people that live very close to the Mississippi River, and I don't take that responsibility lightly. Now that I serve as the President of this fine organization of men and women, every decision I make, is met with huge consequences that effect hundreds if not thousands of people. My mission in making these decisions is to surround myself with wise council, and weigh every decision I make asking God to work through me for the benefit of all.

Therefore, when we encounter these challenges, and we will, why would you lean on your own very finite knowledge and wisdom, and not lean into the infinite wisdom of God? Every day I wake up, I ask God, how would you like to use me today for your good? Asking this question, and actually allowing God to guide your day in every decision you make, is putting your life into God's hands, and not yours. The ability to do this is truly a gift from God. **(Captain Michael Bopp)**

So I invite you to start your day off with a Bible reading and to pray this prayer with me each day, in order that you may seek God's wisdom for your life and for those you serve.

Dear Heavenly Father,

I ask YOU today, please grant me YOUR wisdom. With YOUR power Holy Spirit, please put YOUR words in my heart, in my mind, and on my mouth.

In Jesus name,
Amen.

Bibliography

Covey, Stephen R. *The 7 Habits of Highly Effective People,* New York: Simon & Schuster (1989) p235.

Isaacson, Walter. *Steve Jobs.* New York: Simon & Schuster (2011).

Lewis, C.S. *The Problem of Pain.* New York: HarperCollins, (1940,1996), 91.

Livera, Giovanni. *Live a Thousand Years.* Giovanni Experiences (2004).

Maxwell, John C. *Developing the Leader Within You Workbook.* Thomas Nelson (2001).

Miller, Donald. *Building a Storybrand* Harper. Collins Leadership (2017).

Netflix *Chef's Table* Episode. April 2015

Voss, Chris. *Never Split the Difference* London: Random House (2016) p16.

SPECIAL THANKS TO:

Ana Nebeker (My wife)
Geaux Smile Photography
www.geauxsmilephotography.com

Gregg Tepper
The Tepper Group, Realtors
www.tgroup.kw.com

Captain Michael Bopp
Crescent River Port Pilot's Association, President
www.crescentpilots.com

Stephanie Weeks, "The Lending Lady"
The Weeks Team
www.weeksteam.com

Nicole Azzi
Bayou Yoga
www.dobayouyoga.com

Shawn Blair
Nutrition Revolution
www.nutritionrevolutionnc.com

Eric Schwefel
Schwefel Strength
www.schwefelstrength.net

Pastor Aaron Robison
Fairview Lutheran Church
www.fairviewlutheran.com

Joel Treadwell
Fine Portraiture
www.joeltreadwell.com

James Samaritan
www.jamessamaritan.org

Jack Branch
Branch Wealth Strategies
www.branchwealthstrategies.com

Celeste Marcussen Hart
Creating U Modeling & Talent Agency
www.creatingu.com

Indy, Noah, and Micah Nebeker

Versailles and Jhomer Nebeker

Dr. Bobby Rodwig
Ochsner Health System
New Orleans, Louisiana
Medical Director, Transfusion Medicine

Pam Est Là
2 Corazones Tango Accademia
Rimini, Italy

Nick LaRocca
Keller Williams Realty
Mandeville, Louisiana

Gary Moore
Bar M Homestead

Fire Chief Sergio Alvarado

Chad Goulas

Doyleen White

Joshua Pines

Paul Schaefer

Savannah and Jamil Evans

Chris Keyes

Wisconsin Dave

Will Cullen and Sam the Dog

William McCaleb

Brett Lamarque

Stephen F. Venturini Jr.

Bronwyn Land Planchard

CPSIA information can be obtained
at www.ICGtesting.com
Printed in the USA
BVHW092358150421
605036BV00010B/1467